RAILS ACROSS THE LAND

By Kenody J. Charlton

*Freight and passenger trains
of the 40s and 50s*

Edited and Designed by Debra Keaton Incardone

Library of Congress Catalog Card Number: 91-71585
ISBN 0-911581-22-7

First Edition
Printed in the United States of America

Heimburger House Publishing Company
7236 W. Madison Street
Forest Park, IL 60130

Contents

DEDICATION

This book is dedicated to Stuart Struever, friend and colleague, who shared my love of trains in those early years, and who was by my side when I first witnessed that impossibility—the Hooppole, Yorktown and Tampico.

Preface

I suppose that the young boys of today are still somewhat taken by the sight and sound of trains and locomotives. Yet, when I was young, the spectacle was so very different across the land. Today's generic diesel locomotives and non-entity Amtrak trains clearly leave much to be desired from a spectator's point of view. Steam engines drew awe and wonder from a boy in my day. Who could not help but be impressed by the smoke, steam, smell and sound of such spectacular machines? And the then-new diesel locomotives were so very colorful as a diversion.

The years which this book covers, 1945-1952, were really the last true years of railroading in the old tradition. Steam was still king, and the diesel began to make itself known as a fancy partner, never a threat to steam.

My railroading experience began at the tender age of 14. Like many boys, I liked to watch trains in my hometown of LaSalle, Illinois, but what really seemed to move me was lying in bed at night and listening to the sound spectacle of an Illinois Central coal train fighting up the grade a few miles away, or a Rock Island passenger train rushing along the Illinois River Valley. Whistles in the night had a very special attraction for me.

Soon, it wasn't enough to just witness railroading so I began a hobby of photographing its wonder. It became a passion and a hobby of love. I spent the next few years compiling a visual record of railroading during this exciting period of years. In this book I recall this glorious railroad era.

* * * * * * *

All of the black and white photographs in this book were taken by me between 1945-1952. The color photographs that I took were taken a few years later. The photographs in Chapter 16 were taken in June, 1989.

This book is not a definitive or historical study of railroads during those years. It is not a book of technical information on motive power; nor is it a volume of high caliber camera studies. This book *is* a pleasant and nostalgic reflection on the glory of those wonderful years in railroading, a great chapter in America's not-so-distant past.

Above all, this is a book for those who can remember .... and for those who never knew.

Kenody J. Charlton
July, 1991

Chapter One
Home Rails

D uring those early years when I read the various rail magazines, one thing bothered me. The great majority of photos, it seemed, were taken in the far West or East, among mountains, hills and valleys. It was as if railroading alone was not enough, but that it had to be shown amidst spectacular scenery. Fiercely proud of my Midwestern heritage, I felt that too few photos were presented of railroading in the great flatlands.

Illinois was, and still is, one of the great railroad states in the nation, if for no other reason than because of the sheer number of rail lines within its borders. Aside from Chicago, rail capital of the world, Illinois itself is crisscrossed with a myriad of tracks.

During the '40s it was impossible to drive 20 miles without crossing at least two or three rail lines. Some were high speed main lines, and many more were branch lines. An evening drive almost anywhere in my part of the state revealed an engine shuffling about a country grain elevator.

Naturally, my first rail photo efforts were taken in and about my hometown of La Salle. While La Salle was not a rail hot spot, it was very interesting. The main line of the Rock Island (R.I.P.) came through La Salle, and the "Rock" became my favorite railroad. With its diesel-powered *Rockets* and fast freights hauled by big, handsome 4-8-4s, the Rock Island was all that I could ask for.

ROCK'S 'SPLIT ROCK'
An interesting spot on the Rock Island, Split Rock, was located a few miles east of La Salle. Here, two massive granite hulks from the glacial age lay about 200 feet apart, one on the north and one on the south. Between the two rocks ran the Illinois-Michigan Canal and a towpath road. There was only enough space between the north rock and the canal for one track of Rock Island's double tracked main line, and this was used as the eastbound main. A tunnel was bored through the north rock for the westbound main, and "Split Rock Tunnel" became one the of the few railroad tunnels in Illinois.

During the early '40s, by filling in part of the unused canal, space was made for both tracks to skirt the giant rock and the tunnel was abandoned. In earlier years, the Illinois Valley Railway (to become the Illinois Valley Division of the Illinois Traction System), an electric interurban line, ascended the north rock and angled over the Rock Island and the canal to the south rock before descending again to grade level on its route to Utica and Ottawa. The electric line was abandoned in the '30s,

Ninety-nine miles and 92 minutes since departing Chicago's Loop, Rock Island's *Des Moines Rocket* pauses in the evening at La Salle, Illinois in 1946 behind an E-6. As the evening fades into darkness #505 will soon be off for Davenport, Iowa City and Des Moines, streaking across the prairie lands at speeds as high as 90 mph.

Rock Island's luxurious *Golden State* races eastbound past the Spring Valley, Illinois station in the summer of 1948. Between Bureau and Morris, Rock Island's main line followed the scenic Illinois River valley along backwater ponds and under limestone cliffs.

One of Rock Island's rare F-2s, #42 idles on the servicing track at the Silvis, Illinois engine terminal in 1948. The three units packed 4500 hp; Rock Island purchased 11 F-2s in 1946 from EMD.

but evidence of its existence can still be found at Split Rock. Like the Illinois Valley Railway, the Rock Island is now but a memory, but the tunnel still remains.

BURLINGTON PASSES THROUGH

The Zearing-Streator branch of the Chicago, Burlington & Quincy passed through La Salle. One or two freights a day were run, usually with light 2-8-2s as power. A daily passenger roundtrip was normally made with a gas-electric motor car (doodlebug), but occasionally the unit was laid up for repairs and the schedule was maintained by steam, usually a venerable Pacific and a coach. The Burlington maintained a two-stall enginehouse and turntable in town.

The La Salle and Bureau County Railroad was a small industrial shortline with headquarters in La Salle. The line ran from La Salle to Ladd, Illinois. In the late '30s, steam on the road was replaced by diesel switchers, and I never saw steam on the LS&BC.

The final railroad in La Salle was Illinois Central's long mid-state freight line between Freeport and Centralia. An active coal-hauling line, it approached La Salle from the south over a mile-long bridge that crossed the Illinois River. In the La Salle yard, the resident local switch engine (an 0-8-0), would couple on to the rear of all northbound freights as a pusher to assist the usual 2-8-2 on its climb up the grade out of the river valley.

Fifteen miles north of La Salle was Mendota. Here ran the busy main line of the Burlington, always a good location for rail photography in the '40s with a splendid mix of steam and diesel.

Alco DL-109 #621 leads the six cars of Rock Island's *Des Moines Rocket* through Bureau, Illinois in 1945. The Rock owned four of these 2000 hp Alcos, #621-624. The #621 was nicknamed *Christine*.

E-6 #630 poses for a night photo with the *Peoria Rocket* at La Salle, Illinois in 1950. She's making two daily round-trips between Peoria and Chicago at this time, and as late as 1974 will still remain on the roster for commuter and excursion duties, well after all of her EMD sisters were gone.

Burlington's four-unit FT #117 makes a stop in Mendota, Illinois in 1948 with 84 cars of westbound freight. The road owned 64 of these husky freight haulers and used them mostly on main line traffic, although I was astounded one day in 1950 to spot a four-unit FT on the light Zearing-Streator (Illinois) branch.

BELOW. Another view of FT #117 at Mendota, Illinois. She paused a few minutes for a red block signal, but now has the green and the slack begins to bang down the length of her train as 5400 hp surges under the signal bridge. In a few moments #117 will be cracking the whip with her manifest down the speedway to Galesburg.

LEFT. Another Burlington FT#159 at Galesburg, Illinois in 1949. She prepares to lead a freight up the Galesburg-Savanna line.

BELOW. Rock Island's N-78 class 2-10-2 #3014 on the ready track at Silvis, Illinois in May, 1948 after Class II inspection, minor repair and a new paint job. Built by Brooks in 1920, her class exerted 77,700 pounds of tractive effort, the highest of any Rock Island class of locomotive. In a year, #3014 would be retired and scrapped soon afterwards as the Rock began to dieselize in earnest.

In an unplanned, lucky photo, one of Rock Island's 4000 series 4-8-2s roars through La Salle, Illinois in 1946 with an eastbound redball freight just as the westbound *Des Moines Rocket* passes. Rock Island's Mountain types were uncommon on heavy freight across the Illinois Division; most such assignments went to 5000 or 5100 class Northerns.

BELOW. Illinois Central drama in the evening at La Salle, Illinois in 1944. One of IC's familiar Mikados fights her way to the crest of the grade out of the Illinois River valley with 60 hoppers of southern Illinois coal. At the rear of the train the local 0-8-0 switcher adds its power in pusher service until the crest is reached, then drops off and coasts back to the La Salle yards. The resident switcher at La Salle assisted all northbound tonnage since IC used nothing heavier than Mikados on this mid-Illinois freight line.

Gulf, Mobile and Ohio F-3 #807-B heads a three-unit freight diesel lashup on the servicing track at Bloomington, Illinois in 1949. The #807-B was one of many former Alton locomotives taken over by GM&O when the two roads merged. Located here at Bloomington was the huge complex of former Alton shops and main locomotive terminal of the system.

Chapter Two

Rails Among the Cornstalks

Within a 50 mile corridor of my home in the '40s, many busy main lines streaked their way westward, including the Rock Island, Burlington, Santa Fe, Milwaukee and the NorthWestern. Thus, it was to be expected that my early photo sessions were made on these lines.

In addition, there were several cities in Central Illinois which were of particular interest for a rail buff to visit. I was fortunate to have my good friend, Stuart Struever, share my hobby and rail adventures during those years. Stu was later to become justly famous as an archeologist. In the first couple of years when we were too young to drive, most of our rail photo trips were made by thumb (some in sub-freezing weather). Later, we sometimes used the family car when permitted by understanding parents.

KANKAKEE

Kankakee lay 54 miles south of Chicago on Illinois Central's main line. All of IC's crack passenger trains, as well as secondary trains, stopped at Kankakee. This, along with IC's heavy freight traffic, made the city a worthwhile photo stop. In addition, Kankakee was on the Big Four New York Central line from Chicago to Cincinnati. Big Four passenger trains used IC tracks and motive power from Chicago to Kankakee, thence on Big Four rails to Indianapolis and Cincinnati behind Big Four engines. The connection at Kankakee with its locomotive exchanges added much to a photo session there.

BLOOMINGTON

Bloomington was a great railroad city. Here were the main shops and large roundhouse of the Chicago & Alton (soon to become Gulf, Mobile & Ohio). At Union Station, the Alton was crossed by the Nickel Plate's Peoria branch and the Peoria & Eastern (NYC). In Bloomington, too, Illinois Terminal's Peoria to Decatur electric interurban line put on a street-running clinic all the way through the city, its orange cars brushing branches of elm and oak—and auto fenders at times. The IC mid-state freight line also came through Bloomington. The best spot in town was at Dean Tower Crossing in the far southeast part of the city. Here the IC freight line crossed the Nickel Plate and the Peoria & Eastern, with Illinois Terminal's line only a few yards away.

Joliet Union Station was a well-known spot for rail buffs. At the station, Rock Island's main line crossed the main lines of the Santa Fe and the Alton, thus a busy day awaited railfans.

Decatur was hometown of the Wabash with its huge classification yard, shops and engine facilities. To photograph the Wabash, you went to Decatur, no argument. Illinois Terminal's main shops were also located at Decatur.

PEORIA

My favorite rail city was Peoria. The town was a railroad enigma. In the '40s it was Illinois' second largest city, yet not a single major railroad main line visited there. Peoria's location was the reason for this during railroad construction days. It was too far south of the direct corridor of the several big railroads heading west from Chicago to Omaha and Kansas City, and it was just a bit too far west for the lines building the Chicago to St. Louis direct routes. However, as if to make amends for this snub, nearly every Midwestern railroad built a branch into Peoria. In the end, 14 railroads entered Peoria, including two terminal roads and one interurban.

Being a terminal city, all rail lines, save one, ended there. Unlike most terminal cities, however, Peoria was not inundated with separate yards and roundhouses of each individual line. Instead, the Peoria and Pekin Union Railroad owned the one large freight yard across the Illinois River in East Peoria, and most lines jointly used this yard.

An Indiana Harbor Belt 2-8-2 drags a transfer freight down team tracks at 47th Street in Chicago in 1947.

BELOW. Running an hour late, Illinois Central's *Green Diamond* from St. Louis makes a station stop in Kankakee, Illinois in 1948. It will be hard for her to make up time on the 54 remaining miles into Chicago, for she is already carded at 90 mph running on that high speed tangent.

Engines of all lines then crossed over the river bridge and used the big P&PU roundhouse in Peoria. A rail buff could visit this roundhouse and possibly find motive power of perhaps a dozen roads. The Toledo, Peoria and Western had its headquarters in Peoria and had its own yard and engine facilities in East Peoria. It was the only road not terminating in Peoria but ran through the city on its east-west bridge route across Illinois.

Passenger service in Peoria during the '40s while not heavy, was varied and interesting. The best act in town was Rock Island's streamlined *Peoria Rocket* which made two mile-a-minute roundtrips per day to Chicago. The Rock Island also ran a couple of steam passenger trains to the main line connection at Bureau.

The Peoria and Eastern ran two roundtrips daily to Indianapolis, and Nickel Plate had one roundtrip to Lima, Ohio. Illinois Terminal had six interurbans a day to and from St. Louis and another six on the Peoria-Decatur branch, adding up to 24 movements daily in the Peoria area in addition to freight schedules. Illinois Terminal purchased some nifty articulated streamliner units but found that the tight curvature of the Peoria station tracks would not accept the units. These trains were terminated in East Peoria and one of the traditional orange cars shuttled the passengers over the river to the Peoria station.

LIVELY RAIL SPOT

Last but not least, we come to Ladd, Illinois. Even ardent rail buffs knew not the whereabouts of Ladd. I knew about Ladd, though, for it was only 12 miles northwest of La Salle. During the '40s, Ladd may well have held the record for the greatest number of railroads per capita. The village, a former coal mining town, had a population of but a few hundred, but it was a lively rail spot. The hamlet's short main drag was well stocked

IC 2-8-2 #2126 takes orders on the fly from the Dean Tower operator at Bloomington, Illinois in 1949. It appears as if the operator has his own concrete perch for handing up orders.

BELOW. The last of GM&O's former Alton steam power stands in the scrap line at Bloomington, Illinois in May, 1950 headed by 2-8-0 #2976.

LEFT. On a bitter winter day at Kankakee, Illinois in 1948 an IC local peddler freight scurries in fear from the main onto a siding with just minutes to spare as an 80 car time freight behind a big 4-8-2 roars past at 65 mph. Heads will roll should the peddler throw a red block in the face of one of IC's hotshots!

BELOW. Santa Fe's *Grand Canyon Limited* behind big beautiful Alco PA #53 stands at Joliet, Illinois Union Station in 1949. The PA's snout rests upon RI's main line and she's flying green flags to signify a second section behind her.

RIGHT. It's 7:18 p.m. at Bloomington, Illinois on April 5, 1950 and GM&O's pride, the *Ann Rutledge*, has just arrived at the station from St. Louis. Bloomington is a crew change point and the departing crew wonders what the flash bulbs are all about.

BELOW. Big Four switcher #7214 gets a ride on the table at Kankakee, Illinois in 1947. Kankakee was an important location on Big Four's Chicago-Cincinnati line since the road's varnish used IC tracks and motive power from here into Chicago. The roundhouse served passenger locomotives from this line and freight locomotives from the South Bend-Streator Kankakee Belt route.

BELOW. The end of an era for one of the nation's finest. Gulf, Mobile and Ohio Pacific #5290, still resplendent in red and black with white trim, stands proudly near the roundhouse at Bloomington, Illinois in 1949. This beautiful lady was the pride of the former Alton fleet and competed most favorably in the Chicago-St. Louis competition, matching anything that IC, Wabash or C&EI had to offer, even diesels. This same photo also graces the wall of a watering establishment in Bloomington near the former GM&O yards, appropriately named *The Caboose*.

LEFT. Peoria & Eastern GP units #5621 and #5620 cruise past Dean Tower in Bloomington, Illinois in 1949 with an eastbound freight. The lead unit crosses over the IC mid-state freight line. This photo shows one of the few published evidences of the P&E logo (under cab windows). This logo was never applied to its steam engines. P&E's line, now Conrail, sees little usage today. Parts of it are torn up, while in the '40s and '50s its rails were burnished by New York Central Mohawks and Geep units used in tandem.

BELOW. Just delivered by EMD and still smelling of fresh paint, GM&O F-7 #813 stands a few yards away from #5290, haughty in its appearance and awesome in its promise. Undoubtedly, in the still of the night, a few words would pass between the proven steam veteran and the upstart diesel.

with refreshment establishments whose polished bars still bore the scars of old miners. One of these pubs was famous (and still is) for serving the best fried chicken in the Midwest. I can attest to that.

The Zearing-Streator branch of the Burlington ran through Ladd, as well as a branch of the C&NW from DeKalb to Spring Valley. The La Salle and Bureau County from La Salle terminated at Ladd, and a meandering Milwaukee branch from Beloit also entered the town. Some years later I lived near this Milwaukee line in northern Illinois, and late one evening I observed a freight crew switching cars at a factory with undue haste and loud banging of couplers. Upon my inquiry, a brakeman stated that they still had remaining a two hour run to Ladd and wanted to get there before the pub stopped serving chicken. Thus the haste! Not many railfans realized that the New York Central reached into northern Illinois, but indeed Ladd was the western end of its freight line from South Bend through Kankakee and Streator. This line was later known as NYC's Kankakee Belt Route.

While motive power of the other lines in Ladd was of the light, branchline variety, I was surprised upon my first visit to Ladd to see a NYC 4-8-2 on the wye at the edge of town! I learned that NYC ran fairly lengthy freights on this route to a Rock Island connection at DePue and a Burlington connection at Zearing, thus good size power was needed. The sight of the husky 4-8-2 was matched in surprise a few years later when Burlington began to run big four-unit F type diesels through Ladd on small freights.

There was no turntable at Ladd, but a wye west of town was used jointly by all lines. The Milwaukee maintained a single stall enginehouse in Ladd, housing a light engine which was used on the final 15 miles of the branch (to Oglesby) and on the short spur to Cherry.

Most of the rails in Ladd are now gone, but the fried chicken is still there.

TOP. At Peoria Union Station, Peoria and Eastern Train #12, the *Day Express* waits for her 7 a.m. departure to Indianapolis.

ABOVE. Nickel Plate 4-6-2 #162 rolls out of Peoria Union Station in 1947 with train #21, an all stops accommodation to Lima, Ohio. Two cars was the normal consist of this train.

LEFT. Morning at Joliet, Illinois Union Station in 1948 provided a constant flow of name passenger trains on the Rock Island, Santa Fe and GM&O. Here, in her familiar GM&O (Alton) livery of maroon and red, the crack *Ann Rutledge* stands on the RI crossover as she loads.

ABOVE. One of Illinois Terminal's classic arch window cars trundles across a stream west of Bloomington, Illinois in 1949. The #1202, in its traditional IT orange paint, was built in 1910 by McGuire-Cummings and served mainly on the Peoria-Decatur line.

BELOW. Illinois Terminal's *Fort Creve Coeur* represented the ultimate and final attempt to maintain dwindling passenger service on one of the nation's classic interurbans. In this 1950 photo the handsome streamliner poses at East Peoria station. These streamliners terminated in East Peoria because they could not negotiate the severe curvature into Peoria station proper.

RIGHT. Rock Island F-2 #42 waits on the ready track at Silvis, Illinois in 1948. The brawny red and black EMD freight hauler will shortly be called to handle a westbound to Armourdale Yard in Kansas City.

BELOW. Santa Fe 4-8-4 #3717 comes blasting under Burlington's main line with an eastbound freight at Galesburg, Illinois in 1948. She's headed for Corwith Yard, Chicago.

Nickel Plate 2-8-2 #639 approaches Bloomington, Illinois in this 1950 photo. This Mike and her sisters were used almost exclusively on the Lima-Peoria branch. In honor of her service, #639 stands on display yet today in Miller Park at Bloomington.

Santa Fe Mikado #4083 slams through Galesburg, Illinois on a summer day in 1947 with a line of tank cars heading her load. At this date only about 30% of Santa Fe's freight hauls across Illinois were steam.

Only two months old, Wabash F-7 #1106 was at Decatur in October, 1949 as road diesels begin to replace steam power.

BELOW. Right on the advertised, Santa Fe's *Chief* whips through Galesburg, Illinois in 1947 flying green for a following section. She's 45 minutes ahead of the *Super Chief* on this morning and will stay that way to Dearborn Station in Chicago.

ABOVE. New kids on the block, EMD F units begin to replace Toledo, Peoria and Western's 4-8-4s in 1948. Here, #100 A-B is at Peoria yard before assignment west.

ABOVE. Hudson #700 of the Wabash gets a wheel on the *Banner Blue* as it leaves Decatur bound for St. Louis in 1950.

LEFT. No sooner has the *Banner Blue* cleared the block than 2-8-2 #2708 comes charging out of Decatur yards with 62 cars of mixed freight. She will head west out of Decatur over the Moberly Division.

35

It's 11:20 a.m. on June 8, 1947 and Baltimore and Ohio Train #10, the *Washington Express,* makes a brief stop at South Chicago station. To the right of the station (background) is Belt Railway's South Chicago yard and curving in from the left in the foreground is the track of the Chicago Short Line Railway.

On a cold winter day in 1946 the *Blue Bird* of the Wabash stops at Englewood Station (63rd St.) under the Chicago elevated bridge. Motive power on this day is blue painted Pacific #662, built by Richmond in 1912.

Chapter Three

Chicago: Streetcars and Shoe Leather

In the summer of 1945 I received an invitation to spend a week at grandmother's house on the south side of Chicago. Since I had not yet had an opportunity to take rail photos in Chicago, *the* rail utopia of the world, I was excited about the prospect.

For weeks before my visit I studied maps and *The Official Guide*. My visit turned out to be even more than I had expected. Camera in hand, I set out early every morning for some part of the great city. In Chicago, you could get to *anywhere* by streetcar, or at least close enough to walk the rest of the way.

In the Windy City, a rail buff simply could not run out of places to go during the '40s. For me, it was finally an opportunity to photograph those great railroads with famous trains which, so far, I had only read about, like the Pennsylvania, Baltimore and Ohio, New York Central, Erie and Milwaukee. Chicago had all of the well-

known railroads, and also many interesting but less familiar lines such as Soo Line, Chicago Great Western, Nickel Plate, Chicago and Eastern Illinois, Monon, Pere Marquette and Grand Trunk.

THREE BELT RAILROADS

Chicago also had three busy belt railroads which nearly encircled the city. These were the Belt Railway of Chicago, Indiana Harbor Belt and the Baltimore and Ohio Chicago Terminal. Day and night these lines transferred interchange freight around, across and through Chicago. For electric devotees, there was the Chicago, Aurora and Elgin; Chicago North Shore and Milwaukee; Chicago, South Shore and South Bend plus Illinois Central's electrified service.

Little known and some not known at all by most rail buffs were several rare and all but hidden short lines within Chicago's borders. These were not short lines in the traditional pastoral sense, but were industrial, switching, terminal or transfer lines. Manufacturer's Junction; Illinois Northern; Chicago and Illinois Western; Chicago, West Pullman and Southern; Chicago River and Indiana; Chicago and Calumet River; Chicago and Western Indiana and the Chicago Short Line were all small lines whose mysterious tracks and facilities could only be found through acute study of maps and *The Official Guide.*

Amazingly, the C&WI, a terminal and transfer road, also ran a couple of daily commuter trains, the only such oddity in the nation. More surprisingly, these trains were hauled by 2-6-0 Mogul engines, locomotives more common on a country branch line than deep inside the heart of Chicago. In 1946 there were 33 railroads in Chicago, by far the greatest number of any city in the world, and all had yards and engine facilities.

In the '40s Chicago had six downtown train stations: Union, NorthWestern, Dearborn, Grand Central, LaSalle Street and Illinois Central, plus two other important stations on the south side. The latter were "big"

Englewood and "little" Englewood. Big Englewood, at 63rd and State streets, was famous as one of the nation's premier train watching spots. All trains of the New York Central, Pennsylvania, Nickel Plate and Rock Island stopped here, and the great passenger fleets of the NYC and Pennsy put on a thrilling show early every morning and late afternoon.

Little Englewood Station was also on 63rd Street a few blocks west of big Englewood. Although not as well documented or visited by nationally famous trains as the other Englewood, this station was exciting for rail buffs to visit because of the smaller railroads that used it. All passenger trains of Erie, Monon, Wabash, C&EI and C&WI stopped here.

76th AND HALSTED

The great appeal of Chicago for a rail buff, aside from the stations, was that there were *so many* junctions, crossings and shared trackage locations. My favorite location was near 76th and Halsted, only a block from grandmother's house. Here ran a busy multi-track line owned by C&WI and used by Erie, Monon, C&EI and

Chicago and Western Indiana switcher #234 looks like a fox in a hole as it rests on C&WI's all but hidden engine track near Dearborn Station in 1945. #234's duties include switching Dearborn's passenger, mail and express cars.

C&WI. At this spot the Wabash came in from the west and joined this trackage.

Curving in from the west was the Belt Railway of Chicago with its four-tracked main line, an incredibly busy railroad in the '40s. The "Belt" ran freights past this location almost on a streetcar frequency. As one freight passed, smoke could be seen in the distance from a following train. I witnessed times when all four tracks were occupied at the 76th Street curve. The Belt used husky 0-8-0s on its hauls. Pere Marquette used Belt tracks in this area as well, and its great Berkshires were seen in action here.

After my stay in Chicago, I left with a shoebox full of film, a pocketful of streetcar tokens and a worn out pair of shoes.

RIGHT. Nickel Plate 4-6-4 #177 moments away from leaving LaSalle St. Station with train #8 to Buffalo in 1947.

BELOW. Monon's first venture into dieselization was the purchase of EMD 1500 hp BL-2s. Here is #31 at Hammond, Indiana yard in 1949.

The *Dixie Limited* of Chicago and Eastern Illinois is just a few minutes out of Dearborn Station at 21st St. in 1950. Now curving south, E unit #1406 has just crossed the Pennsylvania main line (right foreground) and will bang over the tracks (center) of Santa Fe and IC's Iowa division. The tower behind #1406 is Pennsylvania's bridge over the Chicago River, while to the right, behind the building, is the raised B&OCT bridge which carries trains of B&O, Soo, PM and CGW into Grand Central Station.

One of Erie's big Berkshires, #3334, is checked over at Hammond, Indiana yard in 1949. These 2-8-4s were the finest freight power on the Erie.

BELOW. Resplendent in red and white paint scheme, new EMD passenger units of the Monon sit on the servicing track just south of Dearborn Station in 1950.

Pennsy's Q-2 freight loco #6181 simmers on the service track at 55th St. yard in 1948. The big 4-4-6-4s developed 115,800 lbs of tractive effort with booster and weighed in (with tender) at 1,049,100 pounds!

BELOW. C&EI's new *Meadowlark* pauses at Englewood amidst a snow storm in 1947. Motive power is one of the road's brand new E-7s, #1102. The spiffy *Meadowlark* began its trek to Chicago at Cypress in deepest southern Illinois.

Missouri Pacific at Blue Island, Illinois in 1948? Not really, because just-built EMD MP freight diesel #561 is being hauled in a transfer freight by a B&OCT 2-8-2 in reverse operation. B&OCT had access to EMD's La Grange works and often hauled brand new diesels with venerable 2-8-2s and 0-8-0s.

F-7 units tack on to a Chicago Great Western consist at Chicago Transfer Yard in 1947. In following years CGW made a normal practice of lashing up as many as six or seven of these units on through freights.

Phase IV F-3 #9013 of the Grand Trunk Western has just brought a freight in from Port Huron, Michigan and now rests near the Kedzie Ave. roundhouse in 1948 as diesels began to handle some GTW freight hauls at this date.

U-3-b 4-8-4 #6315 of Grand Trunk rests between assignments at Elsdon Yard on the near west side of Chicago. This class of Northern was used both in freight and passenger service.

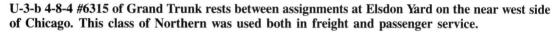

Green and gold and one of America's most handsome streamlined steam locomotives, GTW U-4-b #6408 awaits her departure with the *Maple Leaf* at Dearborn Station on June 21, 1947. The *Maple Leaf* was a heavy Chicago-Toronto consist but these big Northerns could handle the schedule with ease.

LEFT. The *Meadowlark* of C&EI throws semaphores into action at 75th St. as she heads inbound in 1948. Multiple trackage here was also used by Monon, Wabash, Erie & C&WI.

RIGHT. C&EI Pacific #432 rolls southbound under the elevated and into "little" Englewood Station in 1946. She's on the point of the *Dixieland* on this day. In the left background stands the historic Englewood theater.

LEFT. In 1947 a southbound Illinois Central Mikado with a Randolph St. transfer job trundles past the observation coach of the *Louisiane* at Woodlawn Station (63rd St.) The *Louisiane* has stopped briefly at Woodlawn before completing its New Orleans-Chicago run at Central Station downtown. On this date IC is still mostly steam and, happily, on the point of the passenger train is a 4-8-2.

Erie's inbound *Lake Cities* poses for her portrait at Englewood behind three units of EMD power in 1947. It's early evening in Chicago and the platform lights have been on for an hour.

Massive Q-2 4-4-6-4 #6175 of the Pennsylvania eases along the eastbound freight track at South Chicago in 1947. #6175 will handle this time freight to Crestline, Ohio.

It's 8:30 a.m., July 18, 1946 and an Erie 4-6-2 arrives at Englewood with the outbound *Midlander.* Over on the inbound track, the *Erie Limited* running an hour late, prepares to head for Dearborn Station.

Monon's train #5 for Louisville picks up speed near 95th St. behind venerable Pacific #445 in 1946. Train #5 is Monon's single daily varnish to Louisville and it's unhurried pace down through Indiana will bring her into Louisville in the evening after an all day journey.

A crew member climbs aboard F-3 #62 of the Monon in 1948 as the southbound freight prepares to leave Hammond, Indiana yard.

ABOVE. Pere Marquette's train #6 to Grand Rapids waits for the last of the express and baggage to be loaded as she lurks in Grand Central Station in 1947. Motive power on this day is E-7 #104.

ABOVE. The *Washington Express* of the B&O stands on throat tracks of Grand Central Station just before departure in 1947. The length of this standard heavy varnish puts the EMD motive power far outside of the station and past Harrison St. Bridge (in background).

Another view of Pere Marquette train #6, this time at South Chicago station behind E-7 #103 in 1948, after a circuitous route from Grand Central. In just a few weeks streamlined coaches will be standard on this train, and others, as the railroad introduces its *Pere Marquettes*.

Chapter Four
The Legend of Englewood Station

In the previous chapter I mentioned "big" Englewood Station and its reputation as one of America's premier rail action spots. Englewood was more than that. It was legendary. It is only fitting then to devote a chapter to its story.

The Rock Island ran straight south from LaSalle Street downtown, to Englewood Station at 63rd Street. Its LaSalle Street Station partners, New York Central and Nickel Plate, also shared this stretch of trackage.

At 63rd Street these latter two railroads diverged from the Rock Island and curved into the Englewood Station on their way east. The Pennsylvania ran south from Union Station downtown, paralleling the Rock Island but about a half-mile further west.

THE RACE TRACK

At 61st Street, the Pennsy swung into a long eastward curve to arrive at Englewood. Its four-track main line crossed the Rock Island right at the station and adjoined the four-track New York Central for some 15 miles to the Indiana border at Whiting. This famous eight-track stretch of arrow-straight rails was known in rail circles as the "race track." By the 10 mile point in the South Chicago area, NYC and Pennsy crack trains were at the 70 mph mark.

Between 6 a.m. and 9 a.m., the great NYC and Pennsylvania passenger fleets roared down the race track into Englewood. Combined, train arrivals of the two roads were relentless, so packed were the inbound schedules from New York, Boston, Pittsburgh and Washington. During a three hour span, 26 trains arrived between the NYC and Pennsy. As if these steadily arriving trains were not enough, Rock Island's morning trains began to arrive, plus its herd of suburban commuters on a three-minute leeway. Add to this a Nickel Plate arrival, and it was one busy train station.

For variety, the two outside Pennsy tracks were the main freight line into the railroad's major Chicago yard at 55th Street. In late afternoon the whole process was reversed with outbound traffic. No wonder yellow film boxes were strewn all over Englewood!

STEAM STILL KING

Although by the mid '40s diesels were being seen at Englewood on a few crack trains, steam was still in charge on most schedules. NYC powered its fleet with 4-8-4 (Niagara) and 4-6-4 (Hudson) types, while the Pennsy used mostly its famous K-4 Class 4-6-2 Pacifics, often run in pairs on heavier or faster trains. By 1947

Nickel Plate's *Westerner* behind Alco PA units arrives at Englewood in 1948. It's late afternoon and this train is inbound during the normal outbound flow of the great fleets of NYC and Pennsylvania. To the right are coaches of NYC's outbound *Pacemaker*. How striking these blue and white PA's were on the Nickel Plate!

the K-4s were being spelled by Pennsy's remarkable T-1 class 4-4-4-4s. Nickel Plate used Hudsons on its varnish, while Rock Island used 4-8-2 (Mountain) types on main line trains and Pacifics on commuter schedules. Its *Rockets* and *Golden State* were diesel powered.

There was a legend that at Englewood, NYC and Pennsylvania trains would occasionally race each other from a standing start at the station down the long tangent towards Indiana. On a warm summer afternoon in 1946, I was witness to the fact that such things did, indeed, occur.

Time: 2:45 p.m., July 8, 1946. NYC's Train #68, the *Commodore Vanderbilt,* was pulling alongside the station's eastbound platform behind a Niagara. Pennsy Train #48, the *General,* which had left downtown at 2:30 p.m., was clumping over the Rock Island crossing behind a K-4 Pacific and rolled up alongside the south side of the platform until the locomotive was dead even with the NYC 4-8-4 which panted away some 50 feet across the platform. Each train carried exactly 10 cars on this day, the *General* having a few more baggage and express cars

than the *Commodore.* Soon, the *Commodore Vanderbilt* finished loading passengers and got a highball from the conductor far to the rear. As I watched, the NYC engineer made a circular motion with his hand to the Pennsy fireman opposite the platform. He "said" he was ready to roll, but the Pennsy man held up 10 fingers, meaning, "We'll be ready in 10 seconds, wait for us."

NYC waited, then Pennsy was ready and the fireman threw a fist into the air. "O.K., let's go!" Spellbound, I watched the NYC engineer nod, adjust his goggles and turn to his controls. Both engineers knew their engine well, and there was no time wasting slippage of drive wheels with overuse of power. Instead, both the Niagara and the Pacific bit firmly into the rails with measured powerful strokes. The sound was awesome. The Niagara had a deeper exhaust and emitted more smoke from its stack than the Pacific which had a barking staccato exhaust. The gray coaches of the NYC and the tuscan red coaches of the Pennsy began to roll past at increasing speed. Finally, the last coaches rolled past, side by side, already at 40 mph.

In late afternoon in 1948 at Englewood, New York Central name trains begin the continual parade of eastbound runs, only minutes apart. Here EMD E unit #4001 pauses at the station with the *Commodore Vanderbilt.* Shortly she will be flying down the high speed tangent towards Gary.

NYC Alco PA 4200 is in charge of the eastbound *Commodore Vanderbilt* on June 10, 1948 out of Englewood Station at the same moment that Pennsy's *Trail Blazer* leaves on parallel tracks (to the left out of sight). It will be a race between the two famous trains for the next 15 miles.

ABOVE. Pennsylvania was the only line of the four who used Englewood to run main line freights through the station area; the inner two tracks were for passenger while the outer two were for freight movements to and from 55th St. yard. Here in 1947, an M-1 4-8-2 heads an outbound manifest through Englewood.

No station in the land offered a greater variety of steam and diesel power than Englewood during the '40s. Here, a special treat by the Pennsylvania as double-headed K-4 Pacifics stop at the station with the outbound *Trail Blazer.* What a spectacular show this duo put on as they accelerated out of Englewood at full blast!

Three big units of Alco PA motive power pause at Englewood with the *Liberty Limited* in 1948. The train is part of the massive outbound fleet of the Pennsy any late afternoon. She's running ten minutes behind the *Broadway Limited* and twenty minutes ahead of the *Detroit Arrow.*

Never in my life had I witnessed such a spectacle! I watched the two trains roar down the long straightaway toward South Chicago, the last coaches still side by side in the distance. Soon, the trains became only black spots on the horizon, and then I could only see smoke past 95th Street. I never knew who won the race that day, but it didn't really matter, for it was the most awesome thing I had ever seen.

ABANDONED STATION

Today, Englewood Station is abandoned and decrepit with weedy platforms, but legend has it that folks walking near the station can still hear a ghostly loudspeaker from within the deserted waiting room calling out the great arrivals......''Now arriving, the *Broadway Limited*......the *Trail Blazer*......the *Twentieth Century Limited*......the *New England States*......the *Nickel Plate Limited*......the *Admiral*......the *Golden State Limited*......the *Rocky Mountain Rocket*......the *Liberty Limited*.......''

Someday, I will go back to that eastbound platform, close my eyes and hear the sound of that big Niagara and gutsy Pacific slugging it out for bragging rights.

BELOW. Designed for use on NYC's crack *Mercury* this cowled Hudson has been sorrowfully relegated to suburban service by 1948 as diesels took over on the name trains. Here a five-car commuter to Elkhart rolls ino Englewood. Quite a comedown for one of Central's finest in steam!

LEFT. The *Paul Revere* for Boston awaits departure from Englewood behind NYC E units in 1947. In the left background a Rock Island transfer freight waits to clear the Englewood crossing.

BELOW. NYC Hudson #5405 rolls to a stop on the outbound curve at Englewood with the *Interstate Express* in 1946. After loading, the big 4-6-4 will unleash its awesome power towards Gary and Elkhart.

Pennsy's *General* stops behind a spectacular T-1 4-4-4-4 engine. Pennsy crews claimed that the T-1s were a bit slippery on starting, but once rolling were the fastest things on wheels.

Usually dieselized, Nickel Plate Train #8 for Buffalo appears at Englewood behind big beautiful Hudson #172.

Pennsy's *South Wind* charges out of Englewood on a cold morning in 1946 behind K-4 #5399. The Miami-bound train will be turned over to the L&N at Louisville, then use ACL and FEC to reach south Florida. This shot is proof positive that Englewood was America's premier station for train watching!

BELOW. Less than five months old on November 1, 1949 Rock Island FP-7A #409 rolls to a stop at Englewood with a morning rush hour commuter from Joliet.

ABOVE. Although Rock Island did not have a great fleet of inbound morning name trains at Englewood as did NYC and Pennsylvania, it did have a continuous parade of commuter trains on a 3-5 minute leeway. Here in 1948, an express commuter from Joliet behind an original TA diesel whips across the Pennsy crossover on the outside express track (no stop at Englewood) as a Pacific-powered Blue Island local approaches the station on an inner track. The spots in the photograph notwithstanding, this scene spells excitement and action!

BELOW. Rock Island's *Imperial* to Los Angeles—fifteen cars long—thumps across the Pennsy at Englewood in 1950 behind E-7 #641 in the road's red, white and maroon paint scheme. Rock Island was a great part of the Englewood legend.

Chapter Five
Chicago: The Speed Merchants

While not having spectacular scenery as in other parts of the nation, the Midwest had one thing all to itself...speed.

The fastest trains in America ran over the flat terrain of the great prairies, and Chicago was their home base. Speed records were set and held across the flatlands of Illinois, Iowa and Indiana.

In the '40s, the diesel began to usurp steam on some fast runs, but steam still held the majority of such runs. In fact, many railroads juiced up steam schedules to meet rival lines' competition from diesel streamliners.

Unlike many major cities where trains ambled along to the outskirts before turning on the speed, Chicago was a speed haven. There were several reasons for this. First, Chicago is table flat. Second, many Chicago railroads have arrow-straight tracks to the suburbs. Last, metropolitan Chicago covers a large area. In most cases it was 15 miles or more to the suburbs, and trains had time to build up speed. As a result, there were several places *within* Chicago and suburbs where crack trains operated at speed.

Foremost of these situations were the Milwaukee and Chicago & NorthWestern routes where Chicago and Milwaukee schedules set speed records with both diesel and steam power. Crack trains of both roads ran the 85 miles in 85 minutes, which included slow running at both ter-minals *and* two station stops in between.

While the C&NW dieselized first, Milwaukee stayed with steam on its *Hiawathas,* its cowled Atlantics and Hudsons handling the fastest steam runs in America. I witnessed these engines hitting 100 mph north of Chicago. Burlington's fast trains were dieselized by the mid '40s. Its *Zephyrs* tore through the western suburbs at 70-80 mph.

Later, in the '60s, the *Twin City Zephyr* ran from Aurora to Rochelle, Illinois—45 miles—in 33 minutes, start to stop. C&NW's famous *Cities* streamliners were at speed by Western Avenue, only a few miles out of NorthWestern Station.

I've mentioned the famous race track of the parallel NYC and Pennsy between Englewood and Whiting. Priority trains of both lines were at the 70 mph mark at 95th Street. Illinois Central's fast trains tore along the lakefront on their way south, but all stopped at Woodlawn Station (63rd Street) before continuing on to Kankakee and Champaign on 85 mph timecards. Chicago & Eastern Illinois' name trains reached high speed by 81st Street, and Rock Island's *Rockets* began to fly once past Blue Island.

Division points on all lines out of Chicago were generally 100 to 150 miles away, and these first legs were usually the fastest cardings on the schedules.

OPPOSITE PAGE. Streamlined GTW U-4-b Northern #6408 heads up the *Maple Leaf* at Dearborn Station in 1947. Although GTW trackage was a circuitous route out of Chicago, the *Maple Leaf* will still run the 100 miles to South Bend in 120 minutes with stops at 47th St., Chicago Lawn and Valparaiso.

BELOW. C&NW's inbound *City of Denver* whips along near Western Avenue in 1948. One of America's fastest trains, she has covered the 98 miles from Dixon to Oak Park in 84 minutes with slow orders at Rochelle, De Kalb and Geneva!

We're in a vista dome onboard Burlington's *Morning Zephyr* in triple-track territory near Aurora in 1952 as the eastbound *Denver Zephyr* passes with a blur of speed. Our train will run the 45 miles between Aurora and Rochelle in 33 minutes, start to stop, America's fastest run at this time!

Milwaukee's *Afternoon Hiawatha* begins to accelerate after the C&NW crossover near Western Avenue in 1950. The two EMD E units will make the 85-mile run to Milwaukee in 75 minutes with slow running near both stations. The *Hiawathas* were some of the fastest trains in the nation for well over twenty years.

NYC Niagara #6001 leaves Englewood for La Salle St. Station with the *Pacemaker* in 1948. She's averaged over 65 mph from Toledo across the flatlands of northern Indiana.

BELOW. Rounding the curve at Western Ave. heading north on the speedway to Milwaukee, 4-6-4 #104 (called Baltics on the Milwaukee) releases her super power with the *Morning Hiawatha*. I rode this same train a few days after this photo in 1948 (in the cab of this same engine) and clocked the 10.2 miles between Ranney and Sturtevant, Wisconsin in 5 minutes, 31 seconds! Signs at curves along this route ordered: "Reduce speed to 90."

Pennsylvania's finest at Englewood in 1947. A famous K-4 Pacific is assigned to the eastbound *Trail Blazer*. In another minute she'll be roaring down the historic ten-mile straightaway towards South Chicago and she'll be at 70 mph by 89th St. She's just ahead of the *General* all the way to Pittsburgh and between Gary and Ft. Wayne she'll cruise at 80 mph. The *General* will never see her markers!

BELOW. Train #216 to Cincinnati powers under block signals at 59th St. behind a Pennsylvania K-4 in 1946. Despite running over the slower industrial route between South Chicago and Bernice, this train will hit 70 mph between stops on the Logansport division.

Battered like a knight in armor, a Michigan Central (NYC) Hudson stops at Woodlawn with the Detroit-bound *Mercury* in 1945. From here she will maintain 70 mph running to Niles, Battle Creek and Detroit on a run competitive with the swift Pennsy/Wabash *Red Bird*. Michigan Central used IC tracks to Kensington, thus the catenary in the photo.

At dawn the *Midnight* of the Wabash pulls into 63rd St. (Englewood) behind Hudson #705. Even with a heavyweight consist the big 4-6-4 did plenty of 70 mph running from St. Louis. The seven P-1 class Hudsons were constructed by the Wabash from K-5 class 2-8-2s during the '40s.

BELOW. As an el train rumbles overhead the *Erie Limited* arrives at "little" Englewood in 1948.

Santa Fe PA#78 with twenty cars of the outbound *Grand Canyon Limited* growls along at 21st St. in 1949. Once clear of Joliet she will be at the 80 mph mark to Streator and Galesburg.

BELOW. IC's *Louisiane* takes a pause at Woodlawn station before digging in down the double- and triple-track tangent to Champaign in 1946. Behind Mountain #2410 the train will roll the 72 miles between Kankakee and Champaign in 76 minutes without breathing hard. When diesels replaced steam on this train in 1952 it took two or three E units to match what #2410 could do by herself!

Chapter Six
St. Louis Union Zoo

It was in June, 1947 that my friend, Stu, and I decided to spend a morning at St. Louis Union Station, one of the premier rail photo locations in America, and certainly the busiest. While Chicago had more railroads than St. Louis, these terminated at six different passenger stations, while in St. Louis in 1947, 18 railroads used Union Station for arrivals and departures. The time slot between 7 a.m. and 9 a.m. was incredibly busy, and we targeted this period as our mission. Little did we expect what lay in store for us, and from that day forward we always referred to the station as "St. Louis Union Zoo."

On the day before arriving in St. Louis, we took a bus from La Salle to Bloomington, Illinois where we caught Gulf, Mobile & Ohio's *Ann Rutledge* to St. Louis. Established in our hotel room not too far from Union Station, we spent the evening doing our homework for the next day—we wanted to be fully prepared for the busy action we would photograph.

Using a current *Official Guide,* we prepared a chronological timetable of all trains arriving and departing between 7 a.m. and 9 a.m. After all, we had to be able to identify and record each and every train that we would capture on film.

TRAIN EVERY 4 MINUTES

When our timetable was finished, it revealed there was an average of one train every four minutes during that busy time period. Naively, we felt we had things well documented and under control. However, as we would discover, all semblance of order and control was to be lost, and indeed it would turn into a zoo.

The morning broke warm and clear, and we were at the station throat tracks by 6:45 a.m. feeling that we were prepared and ready for the influx of traffic. Our detailed timetable would eliminate any surprises or confusion. By 9 a.m. our timetable was a useless piece of paper!

The first problem was the unique train operating system around the station itself. All trains approaching the station from the east or west approached on a multiple track east/west axis line owned by the Terminal Railroad Association of St. Louis (TRRA). However, instead of curving northbound into the station engine first, as is normal, we found that all arriving trains ran *past* the station throat tracks and then *backed* into the station on one of two huge wyes. From our location on the axis tracks, it meant we had two chances to pho-

tograph an arriving train, once when a train approached from east or west on the axis tracks, and another as the train backed into the station. The bad news was that we began to lose identification control. So many trains began to arrive and back into the station it was impossible to remember if a train was actually arriving or if it was a train down from the yards backing into the station for departure.

BELOW. Just west of the station, GM&O maintained its diesel servicing facility. In this 1949 photo three types of passenger units pose for a mid-morning portrait.

ABOVE. Following the usual procedure for trains arriving at St. Louis Union Station, the Wabash *St. Louis Limited* backs into the train shed. Hudson #700 brought the overnight train in from Detroit in 1947.

Showing the usual Missouri-Kansas-Texas spit and polish motive power policy, Pacific #397 rests on throat tracks of the station in 1948. The Katy's passenger engines were *always* clean and attractive, and the road owned nothing larger than Pacifics for varnish hauls.

The second problem was that the timetable listings began to become confusing. An example illustrates the problem: It's 8:25 and a Missouri Pacific train arrives from the west. The timetable called for an 8:30 arrival of Train #2, the *Sunshine Special.* But it might be an advance section of the *Sunshine Special* (common in those days), or it might have been the *Sunflower,* due in at 8:20 and a bit late. Or what about Train #10, the *Missourian,* due in at 7:17 and still not in sight? (It turned out to be the latter.) What with trains arriving early, late and in two sections, our timetable was worthless. Yet, somehow, in the end, we did manage to identify all the trains on our film rolls.

MISSED SOME TRAINS

Another glitch was that in 1947 we had the old type cameras which held rolls of eight exposure film. This meant that about every five minutes we were running to a shady spot to reload, and missing a train or two. Incidentally, the myriad of throat tracks, wyes and switches were controlled from Perry Interlocking Tower, and later some kind towermen, probably amused at our wild scramblings, invited us up into the tower to witness the incredible array of switch levers and control boards.

All in all, despite the difficulties with train identification and the frantic pace of the whole thing, it was the most rewarding day of rail photography I had ever experienced. We witnessed an awesome display of passenger trains and motive power, the latter an interesting mix of steam and diesel. In addition, it was our very first look at the famous southwestern lines such as the Katy, Missouri Pacific, Frisco and Cotton Belt.

Highlights of the day: Katy's spit and polish Pacific #397 which had brought in the *Katy Flyer;* Cotton Belt's single daily train into St. Louis, the *Morning Star,* behind a brand new Alco PA diesel unit; Frisco's impressive 4500 series Northerns with the word *Meteor* emblazoned across the tender.

Later in the day, we crossed the river into East St. Louis to shoot some freight motive power before heading home—tired but happy—after our day at the zoo.

New York Central train #24, the *Knickerbocker*, awaits its 1 p.m. departure from St. Louis behind two units of EMD muscle. Unit #4026 stands literally at platform's end.

The *Katy Flyer* of MKT backs into the station upon arrival in 1949 behind 4-6-2 #384. Two cars back is Katy's yellow high car used for express which was always found in a Katy passenger train.

LEFT. In 1949, Pennsylvania's *American* has a Baldwin shark on the point as she prepares for departure. MP diesel in left background attests to the continuous coming and going of morning trains at St. Louis Union "Zoo."

BELOW. Pennsy E unit #5858 has just arrived with the *St. Louisan* and basks in the morning sun. Pennsy was one of a few roads which mounted radio antennas on diesel roofs for train control communication.

K-4 #5480 leaves St. Louis Union Station in 1947 with Pennsylvania's *Spirit of St. Louis*. Perry interlocking tower stands in the background and controls the maze of trackage in the station area.

Alco RS-1 #40 of the Alton and Southern brings a transfer freight into Valley Junction Yard at East St. Louis in 1950. A&S was the primary belt and transfer railroad in the East St. Louis area, connecting with every road on the Illinois side of the river.

Right on the advertised, MP's *Sunshine Special* approaches the end of its run behind big Alco PA #6006 in June, 1950.

BELOW. MP 4-8-2 #5310 rolls train #26, the *Texan*, around the approach curve west of St. Louis Union Station in 1947. The heavyweight varnish began its journey in Houston.

82

It's 1950 and the *Texas Special* is now a streamlined train. Here the joint Frisco-MKT beauty is arriving at the station behind the eye-catching red and silver chrome EMD passenger units. Note the logos of both Frisco and MKT adorn the engine.

Normally assigned to one of Frisco's 4-8-2s, the *Memphian* rolls past Perry Tower behind a Pacific on a hot summer day in 1947.

BELOW. One of the most spectacular sights at St. Louis Union Station during the late 1940's was Frisco's colorful Northerns, their tenders emblazoned with *Meteor* for the name train they were usually assigned. In this photo, however, #4501 has just brought in the *Bluebonnet* and waits to head to the engine facilities.

LEFT. Brand spanking new, F-7s #937 A-B of the Cotton Belt (St. Louis-Southwestern) leave Valley Junction Yard in East St. Louis during 1950 with 72 cars of Extra South 937.

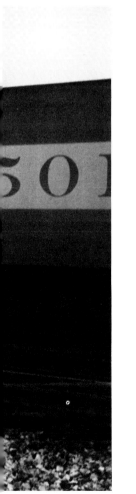

Before Frisco 4-8-4 #4501 was photographed on station throat tracks she arrived with the 10 cars of the *Bluebonnet* from Ft. Worth.

Chapter Seven
Crooked Rails in High Grasses

A favorite subject of railfans up until mid century was short lines. The pure antiquity of engine and track, and the pastoral and all but hidden location of many short lines, made them a delight to discover. Lucius Beebe immortalized the nation's short lines in his classic book *Mixed Train Daily,* a veritable textbook on crooked rails in high grass.

The classical short line was seldom over 50 miles in length, its rails light and usually strapped to the contours of the land rather than resting on ballasted roadbed or fill. Motive power was normally turn of the century and usually numbered only one or two units. The classic terminal of a short line consisted of an old water tank and a decrepit wooden or tin engine barn. Engine turning facilities seldom included a turntable, a weedy wye sufficing instead. Indeed, some of the poorer or shorter short lines did not turn their engines at all, but ran them backwards in one direction.

In all, the main attraction of traditional short lines was their incredibly pathetic state of affairs. Their birth in the early days came about for several reasons. The typical situation was that of a city or town bypassed by the major railroads. City fathers and civic business interests undertook to fund and build a line to the closest rails connection point some miles away. Other short lines were built by mining, lumber or grain companies to haul their products to a rail connection. Still other short lines

were abandoned branch lines of major railroads which were purchased by business interests in the area as an act of self preservation or investment.

Some little lines qualified as short lines but were not so in the classic sense. These were the industrial short lines whose engines spent their days moving about trackage inside the confines of great mills, among furnaces and foundries. Others plied the tracks of huge mining areas, serving pits and quarries. Owned and operated by the companies they served, the industrial short lines were some of the last to die. Some still exist today.

1940's SHORT LINES

For the most part, the decade of the '40s marked the end of the nation's hundreds of short lines. A few tried to stave off the inevitable by replacing worn out steam engines with small diesels, but in the end the profit and loss sheets doomed them all. In most locations nature has hidden all traces of their pastoral occasions. Yet, in the '40s most short lines still existed, and I was quickly enraptured by the excitement of finding wobbly tracks among thick weeds.

Although Lucius Beebe focused on the many picturesque little lines in the southern tier of states, all states in the union had a short line or two at minimum. The Midwest, while not a hot bed of short lines, had its share of colorful little railroads.

Let's take a look at some short lines I grew to know

C&IM American-type #500 arrives at the Pekin, Illinois station in 1948. The 4-4-0 was common at the turn of the century, but C&IM's #500-502 were built in 1927, the last of their type built in the U.S.

Rather like a photo in the classic tradition of 1890, C&IM passenger Train #8 poses but the year is 1948.

in Illinois during the '40s. Probably the best known short line in Illinois in railfan circles was the Chicago and Illinois Midland. The C&IM qualified as a short line by virtue of its mileage but certainly was not a short line in the classic sense of things in rustic condition. The line, a busy coal hauling road, ran just over 100 miles between large coal mines near Taylorville, Illinois, through Springfield, and on to Havana on the Illinois River where it maintained barge loading dumpers.

From Havana the line continued north to Pekin to Peoria. C&IM's tracks were built to carry coal trains, and the heavy rails lay on well-ballasted bed. The majority of its coal trains were powered by clean, husky 2-10-2s, certainly not the typical short line locomotive. Two daily passenger roundtrips were made between Springfield and Pekin up until the early '50s, and were famous in rail circles because gleaming 4-4-0s were the assigned power. Most 4-4-0 (American) engines to be found aywhere were turn of the century machines, but C&IM's stable of three were actually built in the late '20s, the last American types to be built in the nation.

G&GE: MINING ROAD

Another coal road, of far lesser proportions, was to be found a few miles north of Galesburg, Illinois. The Galesburg & Great Eastern ran a modest 10 miles from Victoria to the Burlington main line at Wataga. Its existence was due to the many strip mines near Victoria. Near this town was to be found the enginehouse and a small assembly yard. G&GE operated three 0-6-0s which shuttled coal hoppers between the strip mines and the assembly yard, and two ex-Rock Island 2-8-0s which hauled the full consists over the line to the Burlington Interchange at Wataga. The G&GE was abandoned and torn up in the '50s, but its rails can still be seen in some spots crossing paved roads near Victoria, and at Wataga where the Burlington Northern uses a short stretch as

a spur.

Not to be confused with the C&IM was the Illinois Midland (IM), a quaint two mile line which ran from Newark, Illinois to a Burlington branch at Millington. The IM was owned and operated by a grain company at Newark, and its light rails ran through meadows and cow pastures, hidden at times by prairie flowers and grasses. In the engine shed at Newark an 0-4-0T dwelled, sallying forth only one or two days a week with a grain hopper or two for the Burlington. The IM disappeared from the Official Guide in the early '40s, becoming a private railroad of the grain company, but it ran until 1949 when even the replacement of the 0-4-0T with a small diesel switcher could not stave off the end.

The La Salle and Bureau County Railroad was located at my hometown of La Salle, Illinois. The road was basically an industrial short line owned and operated by local zinc and chemical interests. It ran 15 miles from La Salle to Ladd where it connected with the Burlington, C&NW, Milwaukee and NYC, but its main interchange was with the IC just north of LaSalle. The LS&BC had replaced steam with two diesel switchers by the late '30s, and thus I never saw steam on the railroad. However, on my first visit to the enginehouse in La Salle (which held the two diesels), I saw the old ashes of years past. The line's starting point and enginehouse were located deep within the private boundaries of a factory complex on the east side of La Salle which made photography difficult. The best place to shoot the line's operations was at the small interchange yard north of town near the IC line. Unfortunately, its movements were usually at night, so good photos of the LS&BC were very rare. The railroad was discontinued in the '70s, but its owners, the Carus interests, purchased ex-Rock Island trackage in Chicago and operated it under the LS&BC name. Later this was to become known as Chicago Rail Link.

At the end of a day in June, 1949, Galesburg and Great Eastern 0-6-0 #2 and 2-8-0 #4 are parked near the enginehouse. The 0-6-0s work the mine pits and the Consolidations haul the assembled coal trains over the line to the Burlington at Wataga.

BELOW. C&IM's Mikado #550 at Pekin, Illinois in 1950. The 2-10-2s rarely went up the Pekin line so Mikes were a familiar sight. There was no mistaking engine numbers on the C&IM!

Galesburg & Great Eastern 2-8-0 #3 hitches on to a considerable string of coal hoppers in the yard at Victoria, Illinois in 1949. Next she will haul the train the 10 miles to the CB&Q connection at Wataga. The G&GE was owned and operated by a large coal mine near Victoria. Both Consolidations of the G&GE (#3-4) were former Rock Island engines.

Although the La Salle & Bureau County was an industrial-owned line at La Salle, Illinois it ran 10 miles to Ladd where it connected with branches of several larger roads. In this 1946 shot, one of the road's two diesel engines, Baldwin VO switcher #6, switches cars near the IC connection north of La Salle. LS&BC line operations were often after dark and this photo was made after 9 p.m. thanks to the long summer evening.

Seemingly standing in grass rather than on rails, Hooppole, Yorktown and Tampico 0-6-0 #1315 pauses on track in Hooppole, Illinois in 1948. The ancient engine was built in 1887 for the Burlington and served "The Hooppole" from 1927 to the end in the '50s. The archaic coach was used until 1930 on a 12 mile daily passenger run to Tampico and has deteriorated in the same spot ever since.

Chapter Eight

The Hooppole

It might have been proper to include the Hooppole, Yorktown and Tampico Railroad in the previous chapter on Illinois short lines, but this tiny road in northwestern Illinois was so colorful and outrageous that it deserves a chapter all to itself. Of all the archaic short lines in the nation, the "Hooppole", as it was called locally, certainly took first prize for the most implausible of all.

The railroad ran from its terminus at Hooppole, Illinois, 12 miles to Tampico where it connected with a Burlington branch. On the way, it passed through Yorktown and Aliceville, two communities of but a few scattered houses in the '40s. A grain elevator at Hooppole was the line's owner and reason for existence. On its 12 mile route, the railroad traversed three counties, unfortunately paying taxes to each.

It was on a warm July morning in 1947 that Stu and I first drove the two hours to the Hooppole to experience a railroad which even today we speak about in hushed tones. We arrived at Tampico at mid-morning to happily find the Hooppole's lone engine, #1315, on the Burlington interchange track awaiting that railroad's local peddler freight on the chance of a car or two to take down the line. One car a day was a blessing to the Hooppole. Indeed, the Hooppole ran not at all on many days. Later we were to learn that one day in 1937 the railroad actually hauled a train of six freight cars plus caboose—a record—down the line to Hooppole! The startling occurrence was celebrated in Hooppole by a town picnic and fireworks exceeding that put forth on Independence Day.

The antiquity of engine #1315 was matched only by

the rickety caboose. Engine #1315 was a primeval 0-6-0 built by the Burlington in 1887 and sold to the Hooppole in 1927, while the caboose dated back even further. The engine was locally known as "the dummy." On this morning, local children had parked their bikes on the grass to play on the ancient engine and caboose under the watchful eyes of the Hooppole's two man crew (and entire force) who sat in the shade of an elm awaiting the Burlington local freight. Engineer Bill Durien and Fireman G.E. Renner, honorable gentlemen to the core, appeared to match the vintage of their engine.

Engine #1315 was never turned since the railroad owned no wye or turntable. It ran properly forward from Hooppole to Tampico, and in reverse on the return trip.

LILIES AND RAILS

Eventually, as we waited, the Burlington way freight arrived and delivered a lone car to the Hooppole. Within a few minutes #1315 began to back down the line with freight car and caboose in tow. The track curved away from the Burlington interchange and ran between backyards of local homes in Tampico. Tiger lilies and summer daisies grew healthy and thick between the ancient rails, undisturbed by the infrequency of the engine's passings.

The train never exceeded 5 mph as it headed down the line alongside Highway 172. So slow was the pace of #1315 that there was no "chuff-chuff," the engine seemingly coasting silently along. The rails were totally hidden in deep summer weeds and grass which in spots was thigh high. The rails were crooked and thin with large gaps at the joints. There was no roadbed as such, the rails seemingly resting smack on the Illinois prairie soil. If ever there were ties, to cite Lucius Beebe, they had long since returned to the elemental earth from whence they came.

A portable jack was carried on the tender and seldom was a run completed without at least one wheel somewhere leaving the hopeless tracks. At one point the train passed directly under the spreading branches of a mighty chestnut tree, and at another location it ran through a barnyard, its slowness not at all disturbing the fur or feathers of the creatures which dwelled there.

At one location an incredible sight met our eyes. The fireman had squatted down between engine and tender and with a long-spouted can was oiling the rails as the train crept along. The purpose of this task apparently was to help cut friction between rails and wheels. Yet another amazing situation confronted us as we drove down Route 172 pacing the train. At three locations the track suddenly angled across the concrete highway to disappear into the high weeds on the opposite side. No railroad crossing signs of any kind were posted on the highway! It is most doubtful, however, that any car-train accident ever occurred here due to the infrequency and snail's pace of engine #1315.

TWO HOUR TRIP

It took over two hours for the train to finally reach Hooppole, a pace which could easily be bested by a poor bicyclist or good runner. Luckily, on this day, no derailments occurred. At Hooppole the railroad's three track "yard" was also grass covered, but its proximity to houses allowed a finer quality of vegetation. Unlike the tall prairie weeds which adorned the line along its pastoral route, here a blend of fescue, blue grass and rye gave a more sightly appearance to things. The yard area had also been cut once or twice so that the grass was no more than rail height.

Another track branched from the yard and curved away to a grain elevator a few blocks away. On the south side of the yard a wooden coal bin offered proof that the tender was filled by shovel and sweat. On yet another grass-hidden track north of the yard rested a rotting passenger coach of undeterminable age under which young sumac saplings had begun to intrude through splitting floor boards. It seemed incredible to

The total work force of the HY&T, Bill Durien and G.E. Renner, stand on the footboards of #1315 in the classic pose of enginemen through the ages.

Near the CB&Q interchange in Tampico, Illinois, engine and caboose wait for the Burlington's daily local freight in the fervent hope of a revenue car to haul down the line. Bicycles on the grass belong to village small fry who often play on the old caboose on summer mornings under the fond eyes of the engine crew. Former President Reagan grew up in Tampico and perhaps he too played on the caboose as a boy.

Old boards squeak & groan as the doors of the engine barn are opened on a warm summer morning. Peering out, old #1315 ponders whether to venture forth on yet another day. The junk pile and barn brace-pole testify to the general state of affairs on "The Hooppole" in 1948.

A caboose of historic age stands on a side track waiting for another wobbly trip up the line. Devoid of paint on the outside and decorum on the inside, it was a rolling miracle to behold.

Seldom disturbed tiger lilies grow thick and healthy on the track in Tampico. This location is one of only a couple spots on the line where ties have not yet completely returned to the elemental earth.

believe that the Hooppole ever offered passenger service, yet the 1926 *Official Guide* offers proof that indeed such was the case. A daily except Sunday passenger train roundtrip was made, the schedule calling for a snappy one hour carding on the 12 mile trip to Tampico (not counting derailments). Near the yard stood the "station," a quaint little hut hardly larger than an English sentry box. It was, however, properly adorned with an official "Hooppole" station sign.

Some 200 feet beyond the yard, the Hooppole came mercifully to its end within the confines of an engine barn so old that it must have existed during the time when the Fox and Winnebago tribes roamed the area. Resting in a copse of trees, the wobbly structure was composed of ancient rotting boards. Live moss grew rank upon the roof, while ivy and morning glory curled up the sides. Cracks in the roof were wide enough to allow light and rain through, thus grass grew within the barn itself. It seemed that the building surely would not withstand many more Illinois summer thunderstorms.

SWITCHING DUTIES

As we watched, the crew of #1315 performed several simple switching moves in the yard by use of a stout pole braced between engine and adjacent cars. After filling the tender using heavy coal shovels, Messrs. Durien and Renner put #1315 in the barn for the day. Since the engine was never turned, it was always in position to be put into the barn in proper manner, facing outward. With a groaning and squeaking cacophony of protesting boards, the ancient warped door was closed and #1315 slept, dreaming perhaps of once again pulling the old coach up the line. The Hooppole was torn up in the '50s.

I visited Hooppole, Illinois again in 1989, and I found evidence of the line's tracks and the engine barn on the town's north side...

Chapter Nine
The Great Graduation Trip, Part I

In the spring of 1948 my friend and I looked forward to our June graduation from high school. The best news was that Stu's father had offered us the family car for a 10 day rail photo trip as a graduation present. The trip was to be to Winchester, Kentucky, where we would stay with my friend's grandmother.

For weeks we poured over maps and made our plans. Eventually, we decided to spend a few days in the Winchester area and then make a circuitous return journey, hitting as many good rail areas as possible.

At 4 a.m. on June 7 we hit the road in a Ford coupe. Our plan on the first day was to drive south on U.S. 51 from La Salle to El Paso, Illinois, and then turn east on U.S. 24 to follow the Toledo, Peoria and Western tracks to the Indiana border. We had no photos of the TP&W, and we hoped that our luck would bring us some good shots along the line. At this point in time, the TP&W was dieselizing rapidly, but we hoped that some steam still remained. We had heard rumors that the railroad owned some 4-8-4s, but I doubted this since the TP&W was a small bridge line over flat country in Illinois.

HEADLIGHT APPROACHES

At 5 a.m. we crossed the TP&W tracks at El Paso and saw, far in the east, a headlight approaching out of the rising sun. The train turned out to be a short freight pulled by a Geep, a rather uninteresting encounter. We turned east and followed the track towards Indiana. At Gilman, Illinois, we saw another headlight coming at us, but no smoke. This time, however, we met a lengthy freight hauled by two F-7 units decorated in a bright yellow paint scheme.

Soon we neared the railroad's eastern terminus at Effner, Indiana, on the border of the two states. Here the TP&W connected with a Pennsylvania branch from Logansport, Indiana. As we made a turn in the road, we yelped with joy, for there in the gleaming sun, on a leg of a wye, sat a splendid Northern. Engine #80, it appeared, was to be in charge of the next westbound from the Pennsy connection. A switchman told us that #80 was one of six 4-8-4s still in operation on the TP&W. Feeling good about our luck and the photos we took of #80, we drove southeast to Lebanon, Indiana to find a short line there—the Central Indiana.

Summer sun highlights the purple and white passenger diesels of the Louisville and Nashville as the *Southland* stops in Winchester, Kentucky in June, 1948. She's southbound for Knoxville, Atlanta and Miami.

Just after dawn on June 8, 1948, TP&W's 4-8-4 #80 turned on the wye at Effner on the Illinois/Indiana border and awaits tonnage off Pennsy's connecting branch from Logansport.

At Lebanon, our luck still held, for switching cars near CI's interchange with the Pennsylvania was Consolidation #53, a typical short line locomotive. A little time later, #53 had assembled its train, took on water and began its eastward trip to Anderson, Indiana. Here a real delight occurred, for CI's track ran down the middle of a brick street in Lebanon. Street-running in those days was true Midwestern character. Not only interurbans, but steam lines used city streets in many Midwestern towns. We drove ahead of the train to a location on the east side of Lebanon where the track ran under a canopy of thick elm trees on a residential street. The resulting photo was one of my all-time favorites, and the only one of official steam train street-running. From Lebanon, we drove directly down to Winchester, Kentucky, arriving there after dark.

We spent the next few days in the Winchester area, excellent train photo territory. In Winchester, the main line of the Louisville and Nashville crossed Chesapeake and Ohio's Louisville line, and action on both railroads was brisk indeed.

NO DISAPPOINTMENT

One day we drove the few miles to Lexington to photograph action on Southern's main line and were not disappointed. Southern's passenger and freight diesels in green and ivory were splendid, and its famous green 4-6-2s still hauled all of the secondary passenger schedules.

We arose very early another day and drove to Cin-

cinnati Union Terminal which we found almost as busy as St. Louis Union Station. There was a nice mix of steam and diesel at CUT. The high point of the morning was seeing one of Chesapeake and Ohio's magnificent Hudson types in its orange and silver cowling, and likewise a N&W 4-8-2 in black and red sheathing. An hour was wasted when the terminal police dragged us into an office to explain our doings. Convinced finally that we were but a couple of harmless teenagers on a train photo trip, we were allowed to return to trackside.

Yet another day we went on a short line search in the area. Within reasonable distance from Winchester there were two short lines, the Flemingsburg and Northern, and the Morehead and North Fork. At both locations we were in luck, for we found vintage steam engines in operation.

After several great photo days in the Winchester area, we mapped our lengthy return journey. Our plan was to drive straight south to the Kentucky-Tennessee border which was rife with many short lines. We would then go east into Appalachian mountain country to find mallets on the big coal roads. From there we would go up into Pennsylvania before returning to Illinois.

Our cash flow at this point was a problem, so our budget called for sleeping in the car or in a field, with a dollar a day for food (candy bar and a Coke for lunch, hamburger and Coke for supper). Gasoline took the rest of our money.

Central Indiana 2-8-0 #53 trundles along a tree-canopied street in Lebanon, Indiana in 1948. Street-running, by interurbans and steam roads alike, was commonplace in many Midwestern towns. In the left background, two little girls have come out of their house to witness the commotion on their street while inside, their mother furrows her brows yet again at the daily rattling of cups and saucers.

A L&N coal train marches into Winchester, Kentucky in 1948 leaving proof on film as to the glory of railroading in the days of steam. Joined in tandem are a Mikado and one of L&N's powerful Berkshires.

A spit and polish 4-6-2 of Louisville and Nashville waits to depart Cincinnati Union Terminal in 1948 with Train #29.

A visit to Cincinnati Union Terminal engine facilities in 1948 found passenger diesels of L&N, Pennsy and NYC lined up on the service tracks. The water spout attests that diesels were fairly new to the neighborhood.

Gulf, Mobile & Ohio passenger trains from Chicago to St. Louis were colorful and fast. In the 1920s GM&O trains (then called the Alton) competed for passengers with the Illinois Central, Wabash and the CE&I, but the Alton had the most direct route. *Jerry Carson*

Rock Island Railroad's heart was in Chicago. Here a RI train with E unit diesels pull past one of the Rock's outside-braced wooden cabooses. *Jerry Carson*

Norfolk & Western #2142, a 2-6-6-4, struggles with a mighty coal drag of hoppers at Blue Ridge, Virginia in August of 1958. The articulateds were kings among steam locomotives. *Jerry Carson*

#9944A and helpers arrive at Aurora, Illinois with the *North Coast Limited*. The train left Chicago in the mid-60s daily at 12:30 p.m. and arrived Aurora at 1:07 p.m. Next stop was Dubuque, Iowa, a short two hours away by this gleaming train. *Chris Burritt*

The Missouri Pacific passenger blue, when washed and bright like on this unit, was striking. Trains such as the *Texas Eagles* featured sleepers, dome coaches and a diner. *Jerry Carson*

Grand Trunk Western 2-8-2 #3740 meets #5629, a 4-6-2, in Detroit on September 24, 1955. In the background diesels sit near the sanding tower. *Jerry Carson*

The Mississippian Railway was a freight-only line between Armory, Mississippi, where it connected with the St. Louis-San Francisco, and Smithville and Fulton, 24 miles away. Here in April, 1963, one of the last steam engines in pure revenue service, the 2-8-0 #77 pushes an outside-braced Frisco box car at Fulton. *Ken Charlton*

Nickel Plate Road 2-8-4 #742 is near Hessville, Indiana in March of 1958; you can see the white flags on the boiler. This is a marvelous sight for any railfan. *Jerry Carson*

ABOVE. Chicago & NorthWestern steam commuter trains filing out from NorthWestern station at rush hour are intriguing for railfans as well as the public to watch. In the summer of 1955, these trains charge out from Chicago's Loop to distribute their passengers far and wide. *Jerry Carson*

RIGHT. Santa Fe's warbonnet color scheme is a favorite. This locomotive conjurs up names such as the *Super Chief, El Capitan,* the *Grand Canyon,* the *Chief,* and *San Francisco Chief. Chris Burritt*

Two Nickel Plate Road locomotives—758 and 756—pass one another near East Chicago, Indiana on October 20, 1957. The 2-8-4s shown were built by Lima in August of 1944. The #756 made its last run on June 15, 1958, and the #758 was sold in 1961 and later dismantled by Lederer Iron and Steel in Cleveland, Ohio. *Jerry Carson*

RIGHT, NEXT PAGE. Deer Lodge, Montana on the Milwaukee Road in the late '50s looked like this. The Little Joe's pulled the heavy freight trains over the Bitterroot Mountains and the smaller electrics moved freight within yard areas like at Deer Lodge. Electrification of the Milwaukee was seen as a great advancement for the transportation of commerce. *Jerry Carson*

In August, 1965 an Alco PA powers Denver & Rio Grande Western's *Yampa Valley,* here consisting of only a railway post office car and a dome car, along the river of its namesake on its lonely run from Denver to Craig, Colorado. Trackage is the Old Denver and Salt Lake Railroad. *Ken Charlton*

The Baltimore & Ohio was famous for its passenger trains, but perhaps just as well known for the coal and general merchandise tonnage it ran over its routes between the East Coast and the Midwest. Roaring aroung a sweeping curve at Altamont, Maryland is this three-unit diesel freight, pulling coal and more. The date is August 12, 1953. *Jerry Carson*

C&O's *George Washington* (Louisville Section) stops at Winchester, Kentucky station. While there the motive power, a Pacific and a Mountain, have taken water at the station tank.

Shining in B&O blue lacquer, one of the road's beautiful President class Pacifics is near departure time with the streamlined *Cincinnatian* at CUT in 1948.

ABOVE. Frothing and fuming, Flemingsburg and Northern 2-6-0 #547 arrives at Flemingsburg Junction, Kentucky in 1948. The Mogul is a leased L&N engine.

ABOVE. The *Ohio State Limited* of NYC is behind Alco PA #4200 in June, 1948. At this date steam and diesel are about an even mix at Cincinnati Union Terminal (note steam loco at left). Two weeks earlier #4200 was at Englewood in Chicago.

LEFT. One of America's most colorful steam locomotives, C&O 4-6-4 #490 in her orange and silver cowling stands at the coal tower at CUT in 1948 before departing with the *East Flying Virginian*.

Consolidation #15 of the Morehead and North Fork at Clearfield, Kentucky in 1948 shoves hoppers of clay into a brick mill. This short line was located in east central Kentucky and connected with C&O at Morehead.

Streamlined Mountain #126 of the Norfolk and Western rests at CUT engine facilities in 1948 after bringing in the *Pocahontas*.

Not far from the diesel tracks at CUT steam engines have their own conclave. In this interesting scene we find, left to right, a C&O 4-6-2, a CUT 0-6-0, a N&W 4-8-4 and a B&O 4-6-2.

In Southern's apple green, Pacific 6476 arrives at Lexington, Kentucky in June, 1948 with Train #15, a local to Chattanooga.

An hour earlier, the *Royal Palm*, also southbound, arrived at Lexington behind green and ivory EMD units. By 1948 Southern's name trains were dieselized while secondary trains were still in steam.

A Kentucky and Indiana Terminal Baldwin VO switcher works an industrial area in Louisville in 1948. K&IT was the main terminal and switching railroad in the Derby City and was dieselized by 1947.

Freshly shopped and painted Kentucky & Tennessee Railroad 2-8-2 #7 sits near the enginehouse at Stearns, Kentucky in June, 1948. Within the hour she will head the daily mixed down the 13-mile coal and lumber short line.

Chapter Ten
The Great Graduation Trip, Part II

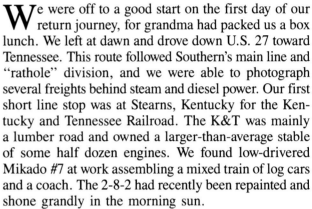

We were off to a good start on the first day of our return journey, for grandma had packed us a box lunch. We left at dawn and drove down U.S. 27 toward Tennessee. This route followed Southern's main line and "rathole" division, and we were able to photograph several freights behind steam and diesel power. Our first short line stop was at Stearns, Kentucky for the Kentucky and Tennessee Railroad. The K&T was mainly a lumber road and owned a larger-than-average stable of some half dozen engines. We found low-drivered Mikado #7 at work assembling a mixed train of log cars and a coach. The 2-8-2 had recently been repainted and shone grandly in the morning sun.

A few miles further on and into Tennessee, at Oneida, were two short lines. The first of these was the Oneida and Western, a 38 mile line that hauled coal, lumber and general freight. The line scheduled a steam mixed train and a gas-electric motor passenger unit.

Our luck still held, for we arrived just in time to catch the daily mixed leaving town behind 2-8-0 #29. On the other side of town was the terminus of the Tennessee Railroad, a 45 mile lumber and coal road. At the engine facilities we found a large assortment of locomotives rather than the usual couple of engines typical of a short line. Most were 2-8-0s and 2-8-2s, but there were a couple of smoking 2-10-2s as well, attesting to the railroad's gradients and tonnage!

The *Official Guide* revealed that a passenger train was due to arrive in Oneida shortly, so we selected a scenic spot in the countryside to await the train. Not only was the train an hour late, but we were very disappointed when the train turned out to be a gas-electric motor car.

BRIMSTONE RR
From Oneida we drove a few more miles into Tennessee to New River, a location where the Southern crossed New River on a spectacular high bridge. Under the shadow of the bridge was the terminus and enginehouse of the mysterious Brimstone Railroad, a logging line whose spectral tracks reached deep into the surrounding hills and forests. At the enginehouse we found a pair of Shays. Before we left, one of the Shays departed with a few log cars, sidewinding its way up a steep grade into the hills.

By now it was early evening and we headed northeast

115

It was rare to find big power on small short lines. Yet, in 1948, 2-10-2s were used on the 45-mile Tennessee Railroad to haul coal and lumber through the hilly country. Here a Santa Fe simmers in the yard at Oneida, Tennessee.

ABOVE. Three Southern EMD F units traverse the impressive New River viaduct at New River, Tennessee in 1948. The lumber mill in the background was home base for the Brimstone Railroad whose track ran under the viaduct on the right side of photo.

LEFT. A Southern Midako has stopped her train near Greenwood, Kentucky because of a burning box car near the rear of the train. The engineer leans out of his cab and the fireman stands on the tender to witness the unfortunate spectacle.

117

back into Kentucky on our way to Elkhorn City on the Virginia border to take photos of the Clinchfield Railroad the next day. Near sundown we came to Artemus, Kentucky, the terminal of the Artemus-Jellico Railroad, an 11 mile coal road. Again our luck held, for the line's only engine, 2-8-0 #16, sat shining in the evening sun, perfectly positioned for a photo.

We drove in darkness to Elkhorn City and slept the night in the car at a roadside truck stop. Elkhorn City was the northern terminus of the Clinchfield which connected with C&O's Big Sandy Division here. We were excited about seeing, on the next day, our first mallet locomotives, especially Clinchfield's big 4-6-6-4s. Finally however, our luck changed, for the dawn broke in drizzle and dense fog. We indeed found a Clinchfield 4-6-6-4 as well as the line's daily passenger train behind a venerable 4-6-2, but the fog and rain spoiled any chance of decent photos.

Disappointed, we drove northward towards Williamson, West Virginia, a main division and engine point on the Norfolk and Western. As we drove, the weather became sunny and glorious, and our morning at Williamson was all that we had hoped for. The engine terminal tracks were loaded with mallets of many types—2-8-8-2s, 2-6-6-2s and 2-6-6-4s among them. In addition, mile-long coal trains behind mallets kept arriving in a steady stream.

From Williamson, we drove north through West Virginia to Fairmont, the southern end of the Monongahela Railroad. After dark we drove into southwestern Pennsylvania where the hills and valleys were alive with flames from countless steel furnaces. At one point, an electric interurban passed over us on a high bridge. We spent 50¢ to hit some golf balls at an all night driving range and eventually pulled into a farm lane to sleep. It was a warm night, and we decided to sleep in a potato patch with our car blankets. We were rudely awakened at some horrible hour by a drenching rain storm and spent the remainder of the night in soggy misery inside the car.

B&O DIVISION POINT

Once again, however, the morning turned clear and we made our way to Connellsville, Pennsylvania. Here Baltimore and Ohio maintained a main division point and engine terminal and also Western Maryland connected with Pittsburgh and West Virginia, two roads which we were yet to add to our collection.

At the B&O yards bordering the Youghiogheny River we found 2-10-2s and 2-8-8-0s, plus a brand new F-7 diesel freight locomotive of four units just arriving with a long freight. Over at the joint yard of WM and P&WV we found more interesting shots awaiting us. I was not familiar with the P&WV, believing it to be a rather small road with typical short line power. Thus, I was astounded to see a 2-6-6-4 on the enginehouse tracks! The drivers of this mallet were white with powdered sand, attesting to the traction problems and grades encountered by the P&WV in the hilly areas of western Pennsylvania and eastern Ohio. I was to learn that the P&WV was indeed

a Class I road with major locomotive power as part of a five railroad bridge route from the East to the Midwest. Its tonnage, mostly coal, was heavy, its route harsh.

Sharing the same house tracks was a Western Maryland Challenger (4-6-6-4) and a Decapod (2-10-0), the latter a rather rare wheel arrangement by the late '40s.

From Connellsville we headed northeast some 50 miles to Latrobe, still moving away from Illinois. At Latrobe was the Ligonier Valley Railroad; we were disappointed to find no steam power there, only another gas-electric motor car which handled the passenger

RIGHT. In June, 1948 2-8-0 #29 of the Oneida & Western chuffs out of Oneida, Tennessee with a short load of coal hoppers. BELOW. Shay #36 of the mysterious and secluded Brimstone Railroad is caught during a switching move at New River, Tennessee in 1948. In left background is the steep incline of track for which these geared locomotives were created.

chores. Now, we finally turned west towards home for the first time, albeit some 500 miles away. At Butler, Pennsylvania, we crossed the Bessemer and Lake Erie main line, and our luck was good, for we saw an approaching steam freight in the distance. The long coal train was hauled by one of B&LE's great 2-10-4s with a similar engine on the rear as a pusher.

By evening we had crossed into Ohio and, at Negley, found a 2-8-2 of the Youngstown and Southern assembling a short train of coal hoppers. Driving ahead a few miles to await the train, we found a remarkable setting for a photo. In a glen of woods and streams we found an ivy covered water tank at trackside. This photo, as the 2-8-2 paused at the tank, was undoubtedly the best of the trip and typified the ultimate short line pose. As darkness fell, we found we had only $3 between us! Obviously, the trip was over, even though we had scheduled some rail photos in Ohio the next day. The $3 bought a tankful of gas, and we struck out for Illinois and an all-night ride. By the time we hit Gary, Indiana, the tank was nearly empty, with still 150 miles to get home. However, my uncle lived on the south side of Chicago and the poor soul was awakened at 3 a.m. to loan us gas money. At dawn we finally arrived home, and thus ended the Great Graduation Trip of 1948.

In one of the rarest photos in this book, Consolidation #16 of the hyphenated Artemus-Jellico Railroad sits for a 1948 evening portrait in Artemus, Kentucky. I cannot remember seeing another photo of this 11-mile Kentucky short line.

On the morning of June 20, 1948 a steady stream of 150-car Norfolk & Western coal trains kept arriving at Williamson, West Virginia behind a variety of mallet motive power. Williamson was a major N&W division point and engine terminal. Here 2-6-6-2 #1412 rolls into the yard with a string of hoppers as far as the eye can see.

ABOVE. A massive Baltimore & Ohio 2-8-8-0 mallet awaits a green signal in Connellsville, Pennsylvania with a mile-long string of coal hoppers. Ahead lies Sand Patch and Cumberland.

ABOVE. In a traditional photo of turntable operation, B&O 2-10-2 #6173 gets a ride at Connellsville, Pennsylvania. What would be large motive power for some roads, this Santa Fe type was small compared to the usual mallets used by B&O on the Pittsburgh-Cumberland Division.

LEFT. One of the largest engines in America, N&W 2-8-8-2 #2112 displays her length and huge weight on the Williamson, West Virginia engine tracks in June, 1948. Giant front cylinders are as tall as a man.

A-B-B-A Baltimore & Ohio FT #103 crawls along the outside yard track at Connellsville, Pennsylvania with an eastbound freight in June, 1948. At this location B&O tracks border the Youghiogheny River (left.)

ABOVE. Although most published photos of Western Maryland mallet power feature the road's 4-6-6-4 Challenger types, here is 2-8-8-2 #909 at Connellsville on June 21, 1948.

A Bessemer & Lake Erie 2-10-4 applies its brute force in pusher service at the rear of a coal train at Butler, Pennsylvania in 1948. On the headend is another Texas-type. B&LE's Texas types were sold to DM&IR in 1951.

ABOVE. While many short lines ran a daily mixed or passenger with the traditional steam engine and coach or combine, others opted for gas-electrics. Here at Latrobe, Pennsylvania in 1948, is #1150 of the Ligonier Valley Railroad ready for the morning run.

BELOW. Brawny 2-6-6-4 of the Pittsburgh & West Virginia cools her heels on the service track at Connellsville, Pennsylvania on June 21, 1948. P&WV connected with Western Maryland here and was part of a bridge route for heavy coal and merchandise consists. The white sand on drivers clearly attests to the numerous grades on this railroad!

This photo, my all-time favorite, shows Youngstown & Southern 2-8-2 #23 stopping at a picturesque water tank in a secluded glen near Negley, Ohio on the evening of June 21, 1948. This bucolic scene epitomizes every short line photo taken anywhere in the historic years of America's "little lines." The waning evening sun in 1948 foretells of the last of scenes such as this, and thus this portrait is entitled, "The End Of An Era."

Chapter Eleven
Eastbound

During this period of years, it was the custom of our family to take an annual summer automobile trip to some far away part of our country. Between 1946 and 1951 these trips practically encompassed all 48 states. This lent itself, in my case, to a nearly complete coverage of America's railroads.

I owe much gratitude and admiration to my father for his untiring patience and dedication on my behalf during these trips. In those days before the interstate highways, dad was obliged to make good time to keep to his schedule. Yet, he didn't complain as I requested continuous deviations from the main highways to detour along secondary and county roads to towns where short lines or roundhouses were located. Armed with my *Official Guide* and railway atlas, I constantly asked for route revisions and delays.

One of the nice things about being a railfan in those days was that nearly every highway closely paralleled railroad tracks. This was not the case when the interstates were built later.

My usual habit on these trips was to spend a couple of evening hours at railroad facilities in the city where we stopped for the night. Then, arising early the next morning, I had more time on the local rail scene before it was time to be back on the road. These annual automobile trips allowed me to photograph railroads from coast to coast.

EASTERN RAILS

The first of these trips, in 1947, was an eastward endeavor from Illinois to New York, Pennsylvania, New Jersey, Washington D.C., Virginia and return. It was an exciting rail photo trip for me, for up until then I had had no contact whatsoever with any of the Eastern railroads.

Our family's first destination was Niagara Falls, and dad chose to take the Canadian route through southern Ontario rather than the American route by way of Cleveland and Buffalo. In railroad terms this meant the Michigan Central way rather than the New York Central rail line to Buffalo. As a result, we followed the Michigan Central main line from Detroit to Welland and the Canadian National main line a good part of the way as well.

In Chatham, Ontario, I got my first look at the Canadian National when the road took us past the depot on a clear, warm morning. Stopped on the westbound main to take on water near the station was big CN 4-8-4 #6264 with a mile of freight behind her. Cut in a few cars back, 4-8-4 #6157 added its power to the train. After both

LEFT. Central of New Jersey F-3 #56 stands in Scranton, Pennsylvania in 1950 awaiting her next assignment. CRP letters on the fuel tank stand for Central Railroad of Pennsylvania, a paper entity for Jersey Central's lines in Pennsylvania.

BELOW. On the same day in Scranton at DL&W's yards across town, an A-B-A F-3 set throbs impatiently between assignments.

Canadian National's Royal Hudson #5702 rolls to a stop in Chatham, Ontario with the *Inter City Limited* in 1950. To the right of #5702 is the tender of one of CN's hefty 4-8-4s, just off a westbound freight.

engines took on water, the train steamed out of Chatham on its way west to Windsor and Detroit, the two Northerns working in tandem of smoke and sound.

Before I had a chance to reflect upon my good fortune in getting some good photos of CN freight power, a whistle in the distance alerted me to an eastbound arriving in town. This train turned out to be the *Inter City Limited* between Chicago and Toronto, and as it pulled into the station, I was pleased to find that the motive power was one of CN's beautiful Hudsons #5702. In capturing CN's finest in freight and passenger motive power on film, the trip had started off gloriously for me.

Later in the day, while driving through St. Thomas, we passed near the Michigan Central roundhouse where Hudson #5370 sat grandly on the ready track. We spent the night at Niagara Falls, Ontario, and after dark I walked over to a rail yard and roundhouse where I spotted a Wabash 2-8-2. Wabash and Pere Marquette both had trackage rights across southern Ontario to Niagara Falls, but somehow it seemed odd to see a Wabash locomotive in Canada when Wabash meant Illinois and Indiana to me.

ARCADE & ATTICA

Our route took us through Buffalo and eastward through southern New York state. Near Varysburg, New York the highway crossed the weedy track of the Arcade and Attica, a 15 mile short line in the area. My *Official Guide* showed that Train #2 was due in Varysburg, but you usually couldn't count on short line schedules. Lo and behold, a glance down the track revealed a headlight approaching! However, my excitement was dampened somewhat as the train drew near: My hopes for a classic short line steam engine were dashed as I observed a small orange diesel switcher on the point of the short train. The train consisted of three freight cars and an orange caboose. Since the *Official Guide* listed the train as a passenger, it was obvious that such passengers who were ticketholders rode in the caboose, a short line tradition on many of the little lines down through the years.

The next rail stop of importance was at Sayre, Pennsylvania, just across the New York line. Located here were Lehigh Valley's main shops and engine terminal. At that time, the LV was dieselizing, and it was depress-

Lehigh Valley owned only two gas-electric switchers in the history of the road, thus I was fortunate to find #76 at Jersey City in 1950.

BELOW. Rumbling along grassy track south of Varysburg, New York in 1950 comes Arcade & Attica Train #2 behind a modest diesel switcher. This train was a daily mixed and passengers rode in the orange caboose.

ing to see a long line of LV's great 4-8-4 Wyoming types (without tenders) sitting on a side track cold and lifeless. Thus, although I was not able to shoot LV's greatest of steam in action, I did preserve on film these magnificent locomotives before they were hauled off to the scrap mill.

Scranton, Pennsylvania, was a fabulous rail town during this era, and a morning there was one of the trip highlights for me. Delaware, Lackawanna and Western maintained huge yards, shops and locomotive facilities in Scranton, and although new EMD E and F units were in evidence, there was plenty of steam to photograph. Central of New Jersey and Delaware & Hudson also visited Scranton, as did the Lackawanna and Wyoming Valley interurban (The Laurel Line), so a clear, warm day in Scranton added to my photo portfolio.

We moved on to New York City. In a Manhattan hotel, my parents planned a tour of the city's highlights, but I poured over maps and transit routes trying to figure out a dawn schedule over to Jersey City where I suspected good rail action would be waiting. Somehow, I managed indeed to find a subway and bus route to Jersey City's busy Communipaw rail terminal and was there by 7 a.m. the next morning.

TWO ROUNDHOUSES

At Communipaw were two roundhouses plus servicing facilities for locomotives of Central of New Jersey, Reading and Baltimore & Ohio. The six-track main line of CNJ, shared by Reading and B&O, was here, too, and my early morning arrival coincided with the inbound rush of CNJ commuter trains on the way to the Jersey City Terminal and the ferry.

A glorious display was put on for my benefit as CNJ's commuter fleet roared past on two- or three-minute leeway featuring a variety of motive power. There were 4-6-0 Camelbacks, Pacifics, diesel road switchers and even new Baldwin double cab-end road diesels. After depositing passengers at the terminal two miles ahead, all locomotives came back to Communipaw for servicing and turning, giving me a second chance to shoot them.

Mixed in with the commuter trains were a few CNJ main line trains from Philadelphia and Scranton, some B&O trains, and several Reading inbounds. The latter included the beautiful *Crusader* from Philadelphia behind the eye-catching streamlined Pacific #117 in its blue and silver stainless steel livery. Like so very many times in my rail photo career, I had tremendous luck during the *Crusader's* arrival. It came at me down the main line at 60 mph and passed a CNJ commuter train side by side for a very rare action photo.

After the morning rush had subsided, I was fortunate to find one of Reading's great T-1 Northerns, #2108, on the point of a 53-car freight leaving the adjacent Jersey City freight yard for points west. Although I was not aware of it at the time, when that photo was developed, there looming in the rear horizon was the skyline of New York City for a classic portrait of #2108.

Washington D.C. provided a full day of historic sights for my parents, but I was off to Ivy City locomotive terminal and yards on a sunny morning. Ivy City serviced engines of Richmond, Fredericksburg & Potomac, Southern, Baltimore & Ohio and Chesapeake & Ohio.

Highlights of this wonderful morning were the classy Northerns of RF&P used on fast passenger trains from Richmond, Virginia. Each of the 4-8-4s was named for a historic Virginia statesman or governor and carried the appropriate nameplate under the cab window. Pennsylvania's main line passed Ivy City, and a constant stream of fast name trains from New York shot by behind Pennsy's famous GG-1 electric locomotives.

LUCKY MOMENT

Yet another lucky moment was in store for me at Ivy City. While walking past the roundhouse I chanced to gaze through one of the smoky windows and saw the bulbous nose of a streamlined steam engine. This rara avis was indeed a fortunate find, for lurking in the gloom of the roundhouse was Southern's PS-4 Pacific #1380,

streamlined for *The Tennessean*, and the only locomotive on the whole Southern system to be totally streamlined with full shroud and skirting!

A trip down to Atlantic City provided me with an opportunity to photograph the Pennsylvania-Reading Seashore Lines, and a mixed assortment of steam power was on location there. The engine terminal produced several Pennsy K-4 Pacifics which hauled the fast passenger trains from Philadelphia, a couple of Pennsy Atlantics and a 2-8-0, which powered the meager freights, on the Pennsylvania-Reading Seashore. Although Pennsylvania and Reading supposedly pooled power on the Pennsylvania-Reading Seashore Line, everything I saw was Pennsylvania on this day with the single exception of a unique little 0-4-0 yard switcher #643, which actually had ''Pennsylvania-Reading Seashore Line'' lettered on its tender. It was the only 0-4-0 I had ever seen, and the poor little thing looked like it was balancing precariously on its four drive wheels.

Next we drove down to Richmond, Virginia before heading home, and on the way passed through Fredericksburg where the *Official Guide* listed the Virginia Central Railroad. This line, only a mile in length in 1947, was a remnant of the old Orange and Fredericksburg, a 38-mile narrow gauge railroad until the early 1930's. At the engine barn, no steam was in evidence, only a tiny and very old diesel switcher #500, which, looking the worse for wear, was obviously laid up for repairs.

In Richmond I had only a couple of early evening hours to spend and chose to visit the RF&P engine terminal. There I photographed one of the line's nifty Berkshire freight locomotives. RF&P had only a couple of these 2-8-4s, and thus they were rarely seen in rail photo publications.

Limited time in Richmond prevented me from exploring the facilities of the Atlantic Coast Line and the

It's 7:20 a.m. on June 23, 1950 in Scranton, Pennsylvania and Jersey Central's *Philadelphia Flyer* departs behind big Pacific #811. She's rounding a bend along the embankment of the Lackawanna River.

In this scene of spectacular sadness a row of Lehigh Valley 4-8-4s sit hopelessly on a storage track at Sayre, Pennsylvania in 1950, awaiting scrapping. These big freight haulers (called "Wyomings" on the LV) have fallen prey to the road's dieselization program.

Seaboard Air Line on this trip, but on our southern trip a couple of years later we returned to Richmond, and I was able to add photographs of these two railroads to my collection. Turning west through Virginia on our return to Illinois, we stopped at Charlottesville, a Chesapeake and Ohio division point. Here I saw my first C&O 4-8-4 (Greenbrier type) #606. Also, 2-10-2 #2950 was in town at the moment.

This Eastern trip in 1947 provided some of the most interesting photographs in my collection. As I never returned to the East again until after full dieselization, I felt fortunate to be able to document the last of big time steam from Ontario to Virginia.

CENTER. Interurban car #38 of the Lackawanna & Wyoming Valley rests at the Scranton station in 1950. This electric line (called the Laurel Line) ran between Scranton and Wilkes-Barre.

Compact and sleek, Lackawanna's 4-8-2 #2227 poses in Scranton, Pennsylvania in 1950. She was used both in freight and passenger service.

Middletown & New Jersey #1 comes out of the barn for a day's work at Middletown, New York in 1950. The short line was formerly the Middletown & Unionville.

BELOW. One of Jersey Central's venerable 4-6-0 Camelbacks throws signals into action as it nears Jersey City terminal with a trainload of morning commuters. CNJ commuter trains arrived in a steady stream, only minutes apart in 1950.

A Reading T-1 class 4-8-4 latches on to 74 cars of Philadelphia-bound time freights at Jersey City on June 25, 1950. So engrossed was I by the majesty of the big Northern that it wasn't until the print was made that I noticed the New York City skyline provided a great backdrop for this portrait!

ABOVE. Pennsylvania's Train #109, the *Speaker*, behind a GG-1 races past Ivy City engine terminal at Washington, D.C. in June, 1950. In the background is a RF&P 4-8-4. The big GG-1 electrics often attained 90 mph between New York and Washington.

Four miles from Jersey City Terminal and both trains still at full speed, Reading's streamlined *Crusader* roars past a CNJ commuter train in this action shot in 1950. Once in a while an amateur rail photographer just gets plain lucky.

LEFT. Reading's streamlined Pacifics assigned to the *Crusader* were some of the most striking in the land. Here at Communipaw engine terminal in Jersey City is #117 in its shrouding of blue and silver chrome.

ABOVE. Dual service 4-8-4 #608 of Richmond, Fredericksburg and Potomac poses at Ivy City engine terminal at Washington, D.C. in June, 1950. RF&P named its Northerns after historic Virginia governors and statesmen. The nameplate under the cab window of #608 proclaims *Governor Henry A. Wise*.

RF&P owned only two Berkshires for use in fast freight service, thus it was a stroke of good fortune to find 2-8-4 #577 at Richmond, Virginia in 1950. The sleek Berkshire carries a sign on her pilot beam indicating that she is equipped with an automatic train control device.

Although this most certainly is a Pennsylvania 2-8-0 at Atlantic City, it is literally an engine of Pennsylvania-Reading Seashore Lines. Reading and Pennsylvania jointly owned the P-RSL, although the latter provided most of the motive power. Consolidation #1267, pictured here, was used on the few freight hauls on the passenger-oriented railroad.

The crew of Chesapeake & Ohio 4-8-4 #606 gives her an inspection at Charlottesville, Virginia in June 1950. These big Northerns were called "Greenbriers" on the C&O.

Although numbered 500, this ancient diesel switcher is Virginia Central's only engine at Fredericksburg, Virginia in 1950. This tiny short line's one mile of track was, in the '20s, part of the narrow gauge Orange & Fredericksburg Railroad.

BELOW. Streamlined Hudson #493 of the C&O stands beneath a maze of catenary and block signals near Washington D.C. Union Station in 1950. She has come in from Ivy City engine terminal to haul one of C&O's name trains to Cincinnati.

Thirty-three minutes out of Buffalo, Pennsylvania K-4 #5418 on the point of the *Washington and Philadelphia Express* makes a station stop at East Aurora, New York in June, 1950 in a classic portrait of America's standard equipment passenger runs so familiar throughout the first half of this century.

Chapter Twelve
Westward Ho

In 1949 our automobile trip was to California by way of Colorado, and it was to be my first look at the legendary railroads of the far West: Union Pacific, Southern Pacific, Rio Grande and Western Pacific.

I suspect that my first real excitement was driving west through Nebraska on Route 30. This highway followed the Union Pacific main line every mile of the way across the state. As we journeyed westward, grain elevators appeared in the distance every few miles, and because of the flat terrain, it was easy to spot smoke from a Union Pacific train ten miles away. This busy UP main line was vibrant with long freights hauled by 2-10-2s and 4-12-2s, the latter an incredible machine with a seemingly endless number of drive wheels.

Our first overnight stop was in Kearney, Nebraska, and since it was July, the evening sun lasted until nearly 9 p.m. on the great plains. Camera in hand, I walked to the east edge of town along the Union Pacific tracks, towards a coaling tower. In a park near the tracks a fair and carnival was taking place. I had an idea.

After buying a ticket on the ferris wheel, I soon found myself on the very top of the high ride. From this height I could see nearly 30 miles eastward along the UP. Sure enough, on my second trip to the top I saw smoke on the horizon. Exiting the fair, I made my way to the coal tower where I hoped for both a 4-12-2 and a coal stop. Half of my wish came true, for in about 20 minutes a long freight did stop at the Kearney coal tower. The power, however, was 2-10-2 #5059, a nice alternative. As it turned out, the photo of #5059 at the coal tower was one of the best of the trip. If this scenario had been on videotape in today's world, it would have been remarkable with the sound of #5059 pulling away from the coal tower with a mile long freight and the music of a calliope in the background. As we followed UP across the plains, I was taken by the sheer "bigness" of UP engines. As an Illinoisan used to 2-8-2s and 4-6-2s, I marvelled that *everything* on Union Pacific was 4-8-4s, 2-10-2s, 4-12-2s and mallets.

GREAT WESTERN

On the way to Denver we passed Loveland, Colorado, and here I found a short freight behind steam on the Great Western, a small sugar beet-hauling line in the area. Great Western was later to become famous in railfan circles for operating steam almost a decade after most other railroads had dieselized. In fact, Great Western's 2-10-0 #90 was long referred to by rail buffs as simply *The* Decapod. When I visited, however, 2-8-0 #60 was doing the honors.

A day at Denver offered me the chance for some time at Denver Union Station. Here I saw Denver & Rio Grande Western motive power for the first time. Rio Grande was using EMD road diesels on both freight and passenger trains to some extent, as well as their big 4-8-4s to maintain passenger schedules. I also saw Union Pacific action in Denver with about a 50/50 mix of steam and diesel. Once again I was amazed at UP locomotives. Even the shortest of passenger trains out of Denver seemed to rate 4-8-4s! Making their daily appearance at Denver Union Station also were several diesel streamliners, namely Missouri Pacific's *Colorado Eagle*, Rock Island's *Rocket* and Burlington's *Zephyr*.

Burlington's north-south line through Denver was literally the Colorado and Southern, a wholly-owned subsidiary of the Burlington. Although the diesel and

In the days of steam no two railroad words invoked more excitement than "Union Pacific." These words conjure up visions of Big Boys, Challengers, Northerns and three-cylinder 4-12-2s. Here are two views of 2-10-2 #5059 stopped for water at the coal dock in Kearney, Nebraska in 1947. She's got 72 cars of westbound freight to hustle across the flatlands towards North Platte.

steam locomotives on this line at Denver all had the Burlington logo on their flanks, railway employees firmly insisted upon calling this line the C&S. In fact, a closer look at the locomotives revealed the small ''C&S'' letters under the cab window or high on the tender.

Moving south, Colorado Springs was the home of the Midland Terminal. MT was not a terminal road at all, however, but the sole single survivor of three railroads which, at the turn of the century, served the Cripple Creek gold and silver mining district in the mountains to the west.

Unfortunately, a foot bridge over a wash between the street and the MT facilities had been washed out by recent rains, and I was able only to shoot a distant scene of the engine terminal and a row of MT's Consolidations. Our route took us into southwest Colorado where I visited the D&RGW/RGS narrow gauge facilities at Durango. At this date, 1949, both lines were active in official revenue service, not yet engaged in concentrated tourist activity of later years.

APACHE RAILROAD

Arizona provided the Apache Railroad at Holbrook, east of Flagstaff, to add to my short line file, but the most interesting situation occurred on our visit to the Grand Canyon to the north and west of there. Santa Fe

operated a 64-mile branch line from Williams, Arizona, to serve the tourist trade at the Grand Canyon. One roundtrip passenger train each day served the hotel area on the south rim. On the day we were there, I was astounded to see the train consisting of 20 passenger cars! Obviously, it must have been a convention or tour special. The long passenger train was pulled by FT freight diesel #153 and three more units. However, a fifth unit had been added to provide heat to the train. The sight of this long passenger special with five units of diesel power heading down this lightly used and light rail branch was one for the book.

A couple of days in Los Angeles allowed me a morning at Union Station where trains of Union Pacific, Santa Fe and Southern Pacific kept the rails shiny. I found a trackside location a few blocks from the station where the approach tracks curved eastward. A short distance further east stood Mission Tower which controlled the movements of all three railroads in the station area. The activity kept my camera busy with the most colorful display of motive power I had seen anywhere. Santa Fe was using big red and yellow diesels and gun-metal gray steam engines added to the color spectacle. Some of UP's passenger trains arrived behind 4-6-6-4 Challenger

In August, 1947, Union Pacific's *City of Denver* awaits departure time from Denver Union Station before its 1040-mile high speed race to Chicago. C&NW will carry the train east of Omaha and the logos of both railroads adorn the diesel's nose.

RIGHT. Rio Grande's tail insignia on this train at Denver Union Station in 1947 clearly identifies this varnish. The *Prospector* is a Denver-Salt Lake City train traveling over the Moffat Tunnel route rather than the Royal Gorge line.

types, and several of SP's trains came in behind cab forward 4-8-8-2s! The use of these mallets on varnish surprised me.

On the way to San Francisco we made a brief stop at Modesto so I could track down the Tidewater Southern Railway, a 50-mile short line under Western Pacific ownership. The TS neither went to tidewater or south, but it was an interesting little line hauling general freight, fruit and produce from the fertile growing areas nearby. Luckily, 2-6-2 #132 was working a factory track as I arrived. After the mammoth motive power I had witnessed during the last few days, it was an interesting

diversion to see a typical short line locomotive at work.

While driving through Oakland I noticed in the *Official Guide* that Western Pacific's *Exposition Flyer* was due in shortly from Salt Lake City and prevailed upon dad to find the WP station. Actually, the WP tracks ran right down the middle of Third Street in Oakland, and it was odd to see a transcontinental train behind a big Northern plodding along a blacktop street. The locomotive dwarfed the automobiles on either side and even dwarfed some of the smaller shops and stores along the street. Oddly, the 4-8-4 carried the number #484, one of only two moments in my rail photo journeys where the engine number matched the wheel arrangement.

STEAM PASSENGER TRAINS

Later, we followed Western Pacific across the deserts of Nevada and Utah, and it became clear that WP's diesel philosophy was exactly the opposite of most railroads. WP's passenger trains were pulled by steam while freight was assigned to four-unit EMD FT diesels.

Our automobile trip eventually took us into Montana and a night stop at Billings. Up at the crack of dawn, I made my way to the Northern Pacific station to await the arrival of the *Alaskan*. While I waited, a short passenger train on a Great Northern branch line from Great Falls arrived behind a green-painted 4-6-2. This was, incidentally, my very first look at the Great Northern and Northern Pacific. It still wasn't fully light when NP's *Alaskan* arrived behind Northern #2675, an engine I was to see again in 1951 in St. Paul (Chapter 14), again on the *Alaskan*! I wonder how often a rail buff would see the same locomotive, two years and 900 miles apart between sightings?

A setback at Rapid City, South Dakota, prevented me from taking any photos of the Rapid City, Black Hills & Western, a rather historic short line. Violent rainstorms on that day stopped me from even looking for the line's facilities.

Driving home across Iowa and Illinois brought me back to the land of Mikados, Consolidations and Pacifics, quite a change from the huge motive power of the West. Yet a Rock Island 4-8-4 and 2-10-2 at Iowa Falls were big enough to grab anyone's attention and welcomed me back to the Midwest.

RIGHT. Joint Rio Grande/Missouri Pacific streamliner #12, the *Colorado Eagle* poses at Denver Union Station in 1947 before its late afternoon departure to St. Louis. The colorful train will use Rio Grande rails south to Pueblo, then Missouri Pacific rails east to St. Louis.

BELOW RIGHT. It's 8:15 a.m. on August 21, 1947 and train #99, Southern Pacific's *Morning Daylight* rolls out of the Los Angeles Union Passenger Terminal curve. No chapter on Western railroads would be complete without a portrait of a big red, orange and white GS-4 Northern of SP.

Tidewater Southern 2-6-2 #132 performs switching duties at Modesto, California in 1947. This 50-mile short line, owned by Western Pacific, served the area's fruit and vegetable industry, and the seasoned Prairie-type locomotive also hauled a daily mixed train to Ortega.

Like a behemoth from the Silurian Age, Norfolk & Western Y6b #2151 ambles along towards the water tank at Radford, Virginia on the Bristol Division in July, 1950. N&W's famous 2-8-8-2 Y6 class were reportedly the world's most powerful engines.

Chapter Thirteen

Southern Cooking

In 1950 our itinerary was planned for a trip through the Dixie states. By this date dieselization was in full swing, but there was still abundant steam, and I was anxious to probe the Southern states where numerous colorful short lines still struggled on. I was eager to tread in the footsteps of Lucius Beebe who glorified the ancient short lines of Arkansas and other Dixie states. Our trip led us through Arkansas, Louisiana, Mississippi, Alabama, Virginia, West Virginia, Tennessee and Kentucky.

We actually drove south into Kentucky first and

stopped at Fulton in the evening. This was an important stop for me, for Fulton was a division point and engine terminal of the Illinois Central. Although the IC certainly was not a new railroad for me, I wanted to get to Fulton especially to see IC's nice 2-8-4 Berkshire types (called Lima types on the IC), which did not appear in Northern or Central Illinois. They were used on the Edgewood cutoff exclusively between Fulton, Kentucky, and Bluford, Illinois, and I had never seen one. I took a photo of #8047 in the rain as she ambled towards the turntable, but another locomotive was an

appeared to me anyway, as if nearly every town harbored a short line, which connected to either the Missouri Pacific or Rock Island. Short line-hunting was exciting and fun. At a town where such a line existed, the procedure was to proceed through the town until the street crossed a light and wobbly track, then follow the track until we came to the railroad's yard and engine facility.

The hope, of course, was to find an engine either standing outside of the locomotive shed or perhaps working around the area. In most cases, happily, this was the norm, except in the lone case of the Fordyce & Princeton where the road's quaint little 2-8-0 #101 sat glumly inside the barn alongside a diesel switcher which obviously had taken over the daily duties for good. Time did not permit us to catch any short line trains out upon the line, as a good part of day could be spent awaiting such rare ventures. Only in the case where our arrival coincided within a short time of a scheduled short line mixed or passenger train did we stop for any time at all. The only situation where this occurred was at El Dorado, Arkansas, where the daily passenger train of the El Dorado and Wesson arrived after a short wait on our part.

A trim 2-8-0 came into town pushing a lone coach ahead of itself and made several switching moves near the quaint two-story station and headquarters of the railroad. For the most part, it was satisfactory enough to photograph a short line's motive power and then move on to the next short line a few miles down the highway. In Arkansas, the short lines were usually feeders to large railroads, but in Louisiana, most of them were lumber haulers, many owned and operated by the lumber companies they served.

NO RAIL CITY

New Orleans did not look like a railroad city in any sense of the word, and it wasn't. Railroad yards and stations should have the look of a John Madden football player: dirty, grimy, sooty. Some well-known passenger trains came to New Orleans but smoke and steam was hard to find there in 1950. It seemed somehow only natural that diesels pulled most of the trains in this southern outpost. After all, the throat tracks and open air platforms of the major stations were surrounded by azalea and palm. It was hard to imagine roundhouses in New Orleans, although there must have been a couple, for steam was not dead in 1950. Be it as it may, I did not see or hear one steam engine when I was there. Some photos of IC's *Panama Limited* and Kansas City Southern's *Southern Belle* were the best of my New Orleans train shots.

As we headed for Tennessee I made up my mind to focus the limited time I had on our stops upon railroads which were new to my portfolio. My quest was similar to a stamp collector looking for new species. Thus, in Nashville, a major stronghold of the Louisville & Nashville, I spent no time at all on that railroad. After all, I had taken many documentary photos of that road at Winchester and Cincinnati a few years earlier. In-

was an important find as well, for it was an 0-8-2, unique to the IC, I believe.

Several years earlier while driving past the IC yards in Clinton, Illinois, I saw what looked like an 0-8-2, but at that time I shook my head and thought that there was no such animal. At Fulton I verified that such creatures did indeed exist on the IC, apparently an IC innovation made by removing the pilot trucks from 2-8-2s and using them for switchers. They must have been very powerful switchers as a result.

RAMPANT SHORT LINES

We drove into Arkansas the next day and spent two days tracking down short lines. Arkansas and northern Louisiana were still rampant with short lines in 1950. A scant few years later, most of them were gone forever, so the timing of the trip was fortunate to say the least.

As we swung into Arkansas, I kept busy in the back seat matching the road map to my *Official Guide*. It

stead, I spent the few hours of free time tracking down the facilities of the Tennessee Central. I was rewarded when I finally found the TC yard, for although the line had recently dieselized with Alco road switchers, some of its former steam power still sat in the yard awaiting disposition and scrapping. Among the locos was a 2-6-6-2 mallet, and it came as a surprise for I never knew that the small railroad used mallets. Before the next decade was out, TC would be gone, absorbed by L&N.

Similarly in Chattanooga, a Southern stronghold, I spent my photo time on the Nashville, Chattanooga & St. Louis and the Tennessee, Alabama & Georgia. The latter road was a rarely photographed 90-mile line between Chattanooga, Tennessee and Gadsden, Alabama. Happily, TA&G was still fully in steam and exhibited a couple of nice Mikados at its facilities on Chattanooga's east side.

Our route took us through Erwin, Tennessee before crossing the mountains into Virginia. I had coaxed dad into routing our path through Erwin for I knew that the Clinchfield had its major engine terminal and shops there. I remembered the foggy, rainy day at Elkhorn City two years earlier when the weather foiled my attempts to photograph Clinchfield's big power. This time, however, the day was perfect as we arrived at Erwin and I had a full hour to spend!

HUGE CHALLENGER

As I walked from the car to the yards I saw a sight which elated me. There, on the point of a long freight ready to leave, was 4-6-6-4 #672. The huge Challenger glistened in the sun and actually towered over the boxcars behind it! What a superb locomotive it was. Yet, steam days on the Clinchfield were numbered for lurking near the engine terminal was the railroad's first road freight diesel #200, only a few weeks old. Engine #200 was the only FP7 the Clinchfield ever owned and still runs today as CSX #118.

Near the roundhouse, on storage tracks radiating from the turntable, sat many older mallets, mostly 2-8-8-2s

Illinois Central's pride and joy, the *Panama Limited* awaits departure time in New Orleans in 1950 behind EMD E units. (IC was loyal to EMD for all passenger motive power). In a few minutes, it's off to Memphis and Chicago.

Typical of many Southern short lines by 1950, the NL&G tried to stave off its demise by replacing worn out steam locomotives with diesel switchers. Here is utilitarian switcher #101 at Hodge, Louisiana.

While marked with a Missouri Pacific emblem, this Davenport-Besler 44-ton switcher belonged to the Doniphan, Kensett & Searcy Railway at Kensett, Arkansas in July, 1950. Having scrapped its steam engine, this 6-mile short line has leased this MP switcher to continue operations.

Consolidation #16 and El Dorado & Wesson Railway moves along a yard track in El Dorado, Arkansas, typical of the numerous short lines which seemed to be found in almost every Arkansas town connecting to the Rock Island or Missouri Pacific.

No photo could be more indicative of the changing of the guard than this inside shot of the engine barn of the Fordyce & Princeton at Fordyce, Arkansas in 1950. Engine #101, a 2-8-0, slumbers endlessly, rarely used, as its diesel replacement and housemate gets the call now for the daily chores.

awaiting the scrap pile. On one of these tracks, surrounded on both sides by a hulking mallet, was an elderly 4-6-0 lettered for the Black Mountain Railway. Black Mountain was a tiny North Carolina short line owned by the Clinchfield, and old #1 probbly escaped the torch. I suspect it was used until recently as Clinchfield (CSX) #1 on excursion and Santa Claus trips in the area. A live Consolidation #306 worked the Erwin yards, so my day with the Clinchfield was fruitful.

Later the same day we crossed the Appalachians and arrived at Radford, Virginia where I saw a Norfolk & Western freight on the Bristol line. The locomotive, stopped for coal and water, was Y6b #2151, my first look at an N&W 2-8-8-2. The huge locomotive, carrying green flags, filled its appetite at the towers, backed onto its train, and got away with a show of crackling sound and smoke.

In a while we were at N&W's Roanoke, headquarters, shops and engine facilities. Mallets abounded on the service tracks, but the most interesting locomotives of all were N&W's 4-8-0s, used for switching.

VIRGINIAN RR

A short trip across town, the Virginian maintained yards. My first experience with the Virginian was a good one, for protruding from an enginehouse, was big electric locomotive #128. Beginning at Roanoke the Virginian was electrified westward into West Virginia and it used steam to Atlantic tidewater to the east. The massive 120 Series electrics were among the most powerful electric locomotives in the nation. As a study in contrast, near the #128 sat elderly low-drivered Mikado #430.

At Richmond I hunted out the facilities of the Atlantic Coast Line and Seaboard Air Line, both roads already about 80% dieselized. SAL's diesel tracks were filled with EMD freight (F) and passenger (E) units in colorful green, red and yellow livery. Happily, 2-8-2 #370 was there as well, still in steam and still hauling freight. On the ACL, only purple and white freight diesel #301 was in town at the moment; I found her near the roundhouse which ACL shared with the RF&P. Certainly the attractive colors of ACL and SAL diesels were to my eyes the prettiest in all of Dixie.

After a couple of days at the mandatory colonial and presidential historic sites, we turned towards home and spent a day at Greenbrier, West Virginia where dad and I had a round of golf. Chesapeake and Ohio's main line passed through Greenbrier, and I was anxious to shoot some of the road's mallet power, especially its big 2-6-6-6 Alleghenies. Unfortunately, although I spent several hours by the tracks, there was nothing moving on the C&O this day. However, that night while at the hotel, I heard the ''big ones'' come through town on coal drags, thus they escaped my camera lens.

MEADOW RIVER

Yet, the next day I was treated to an unexpected

El Dorado & Wesson's 2-8-0 #16 has just arrived at El Dorado, Arkansas with passenger Train #2. She has cut away from the ancient Jim Crow coach and proceeds towards the wye for turning.

pleasure. Deep in West Virginia hill country at Rainelle we suddenly came upon the Meadow River Lumber railroad, a line not shown in the *Official Guide* or maps. Snorting about the big lumber stacks was an ancient Shay locomotive with a cabbage stack! The locomotive was a remaining artifact of hundreds of such Shays used by lumber mills during the early days in the mountains of deepest West Virginia to horse the log cars up and down steep grades from forest to mill.

A final highlight of this trip was our drive through southern Indiana to ferret out the Louisville, New Albany & Corydon. This charming short line ran about eight miles from Corydon to Corydon Junction where it connected with the St. Louis division of the Southern Railway. In the old days, the LNA&C ran a passenger train up to the junction but by 1950 it had been freight-only for over a decade. This line qualified in all aspects as a traditional short line; grass-covered light rails which undulated through the Indiana countryside under oak and maple and across farm lands. At Corydon, near the old station, sat primeval 4-4-0 #9. This photogenic American locomotive was painted green with a red wooden cab, and wisps of steam escaped from its cylinders as it rested for the night. The LNA&C was a grand end to a fabulous photo trip in the Dixie states.

Alco RS-2 #258 of Tennessee Central throbs away in the Nashville, Tennessee yard in 1950. A short distance away, TC steam power, replaced by diesels such as 258, stood on a scrap track, including a 2-6-6-2.

After a brief rain, E-8 #22 heads Kansas City Southern's *Southern Belle* at its New Orleans terminal in July, 1950.

BELOW. The archetypal short line scene is captured at Winnfield, Louisiana in 1950 on the Termont & Gulf; a pair of venerable 4-6-0s, a wood and tin engine barn, high weeds and an equipment flat car. This portrait would indeed have pleased Lucius Beebe.

Rarely was seen a photo of the Tennessee, Alabama & Georgia. Yet at Chattanooga in 1950 I persevered all day to find white-trimmed Mikado #401 heading a brace of TAG engines on the east side of the city.

BELOW. Although the Virginian Railway was known for its giant electric and mallet locomotives, I found low-drivered 2-8-2 #430 at Roanoke, Virginia in 1950. West of Roanoke, the Virginian was electrified, while eastward to tidewater, steam held forth.

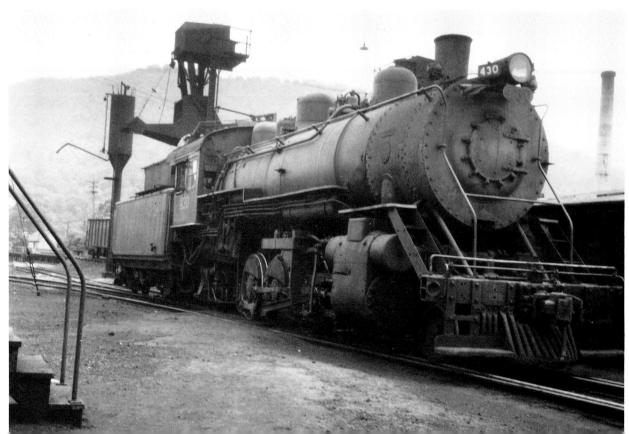

By 1950 even the Clinchfield had begun to supplant its great 4-6-6-4 Challengers with diesel power. Here, at Erwin, Tennessee are FP-7 units waiting to handle the next call.

One of Virginian's monstrous EL2B electrics stands at the shop in Roanoke on July 28, 1950. Here's 6800 hp and one million pounds of locomotive!

The engineer heads home after a day's work aboard Louisville, New Albany & Corydon 4-4-0 #9 in 1950. In the grand style of turn of the century engines, green painted #9 sports a red wooden cab.

BELOW. In purple and white splendor, Atlantic Coast Line FT units #305 A-B bask under the summer sun in Richmond, Virginia in July, 1950.

A mid-day visit to Seaboard's Richmond, Virginia diesel facilities on July 29, 1950 found EMD freight and passenger units being serviced for duty.

Seaboard E7 #3041 stands on a diesel servicing track at Richmond. She'll be assigned to the next Florida-bound varnish off of RF&P from Washington, D.C.

Chapter Fourteen
The Northlands

My father announced in 1951 that our annual summer automobile trip would be of shorter duration and route. It was to take us north into Wisconsin, Minnesota, upper Michigan and return through lower Michigan. After the previous trips to the far West, the East and deep South which produced valuable additions to my rail photo portfolio, I was not too excited about this trip from a railfan's standpoint. What rail interest could this trip produce? Yet, I went to work with my railroad maps and *Official Guide* and quickly realized that there were some intriguing situations to the north, including some railroads that I had not yet seen.

The first stop of consequence was Green Bay, Wisconsin on a hot, July day, and we arrived early enough to hunt out the facilities of the Green Bay & Western. I found the location by using the city map in the phone book. Imagine my delight, when arriving at the enginehouse, I found the railroad still fully in steam. Clean, well-groomed Mikados #401 and #402 were available on this day for my camera—the trip was off to a good start.

The following day we headed for scenic Door County. We headed east out of Green Bay and then north to Sturgeon Bay where the *Official Guide* informed me I would find a short line entitled the Ahnapee & Western and the only railroad in Door County. This tiny line ran from Sturgeon Bay, 34 miles southward to Casco Junction, where it connected with the Kewaunee, Green Bay & Western, a subsidiary of the Green Bay & Western.

The morning was brilliant, the sun glistening upon

In one of those rare cases where engine number and wheel type are identical, Ahnapee & Western 2-6-0 #260 protrudes from the quonset engine barn at Sturgeon Bay, Wisconsin in July, 1951. The 34-mile short line ran from Sturgeon Bay to Casco Junction where it connected with the Kewaunee, Green Bay & Western, both railroads being part of the Green Bay & Western system.

the slow swells of the bay. After crossing the automobile bridge over the water into the city of Sturgeon Bay, I saw the facilities of the short line off to our left, not too far from the water. We made straight for the quonset-type engine barn; our luck was good, for there outside the barn, was the line's only locomotive, 2-6-0 Mogul #260. It was another of those rare cases where the engine number matched the wheel type.

HIAWATHA CONNECTING SERVICE

Heading west the next day, we spent the night in Woodruff, Wisconsin the extreme northern end of Milwaukee's historic 170-mile branch from the main line at New Lisbon far to the south. It was dark when we arrived at our motel so no photos were possible, but the *Official Guide* revealed that Milwaukee's Train #201 was due in at 9 p.m. and before the appointed time I was down at the station. Train #201 was listed in the timetable as "Hiawatha-North woods Section" and made a connection with the *real* Hiawatha at New Lisbon. Its purpose was to provide connecting service to the resort and lakes area in northern Wisconsin.

My interest in this train on this warm summer night was its motive power possibilities. Although the train was pulled by diesel power some of the time, it was rumored that on occasion steam was still used and oc-

casionally one of Milwaukee's famous streamlined A Class 4-4-2s was on the point. In the 1930's the Milwaukee streamlined four of these Atlantics for *Hiawatha* service, with attractive orange, white and black sheathing. The roster numbers were #1-4, and they were capable of 100 miles per hour with a six-car *Hiawatha* train. Later, when the consists of the *Hiawathas* were lengthened, the Atlantics were replaced by the heavy F-7 Hudsons which in turn were later displaced by diesels. The Atlantics were then relegated to branch lines and secondary trains. In 1942 I had witnessed Atlantic #1 hitting 100 mph near Zion, Illinois. But now, in 1951, it was said that most or all of the fabled Atlantics were on the scrap line at Bensenville, so my hopes were not high on this glorious summer night in the north woods. As I stood on the station platform, the sky was a canopy of stars and the smell of pine was strong. The only sounds were the clatter of the telegraph in the station cubicle, the cry of a loon far away, the hoot of an owl in the woods across the tracks and an automobile horn somewhere in town. My watch said 8:45, 8:50, then 8:55; suddenly, far to the south, I heard that spine-tingling wail of a steam whistle. When the train rounded a slight curve in the distance, I knew by the unique high headlight position that this

F-3 A-B-A units of Great Northern move from the yards towards St. Paul Union Station in 1951 to tack on to the *Fast Mail* for Seattle. At this date EMD motive power began to replace steam on Great Northern's priority varnish.

was one of the streamlined Atlantics!

A 4-4-2 #2, under its beautiful orange cowling, rolled into the station with its four car train, proud and swift-looking, albeit on this medium-speed schedule at the end of a lonely single track branch deep in the north woods, a far cry from the heavy double track speedway between Chicago and Milwaukee where curves were steeply banked to accept 90 mph running! For me, the moment was an emotional one under the indigo sky.

Before I left the station I patted the side of the tender of that Atlantic and said aloud: "Thanks #2, nice career. May your dreams be filled with those fleeting glances of Deerfield, Lake Forest, Rondout and Sturtevant as you slowed down to 90 for the curves." There was a lump in my throat for I knew I would never see one of these magnificent Atlantics again—and I didn't. As I walked back up the quiet street of Woodruff, the Northern Lights put on a brilliant display of green, yellow and red in the northern sky. I think to this day that the Father was

saying His farewell to this grand lady of the rails.

ST. PAUL UNION STATION

Our family went on to Minnesota, and I spent a morning at St. Paul Union Station, one of the more active and interesting train-watching spots in the nation. Burlington, Milwaukee, NorthWestern, Rock Island, Northern Pacific, Great Northern, Soo and Chicago Great Western sent trains past my camera lens in a steady procession between seven and nine in the morning.

Of great interest to me were the Soo and CGW passenger trains. Marginal passenger railroads at best, the varnish of Soo and CGW were hard to find over the systems. Yet, here in St. Paul, several arrived and departed in the morning hours. Best of all, I had the chance to shoot Northern Pacific and Great Northern motive power, for until then I had no photographs of either road. GN's varnish in 1951 was fully dieselized, its name trains coming into St. Paul behind three-unit EMD road diesels in green and orange livery. NP was

Great Northern F-3 #260 leads the *Dakotan* into St. Paul Union Station in 1951. She's five minutes early after an over night from Minot, North Dakota.

still a mixture of steam and diesel, its secondary long-haul trains hauled by the road's big Northerns. In fact, arriving on the *Alaskan* was my old friend 4-8-4 #2675 which I had seen a couple of years earlier pulling the *Alaskan* in Billings, Montana.

Later in the morning, when the passenger rush was over, I walked about a mile down the NP tracks to the Cayuga Street roundhouse where I photographed #2675 being washed under high pressure hoses. An interesting arrival at the station earlier in the morning is worth noting: Rock Island's *Zephyr-Rocket* arrived behind Burlington E units. This train was a joint entity of Burlington and Rock Island, using Rock Island tracks from St. Paul to Burlington, Iowa, then on Burlington rails to St. Louis. Originally, the two railroads exchanged engines at Burlington, Iowa, but later they pooled power on alternate weeks using one line's motive power all the way through.

Our itinerary into upper Michigan missed Duluth, unfortunately, so I was not able to fulfill my desire to witness Duluth, Missabe & Iron Range's ore-hauling mallets. Later, in 1970, I did get back to the same area on a vacation and saw one of the massive 2-8-8-4s on

display at Two Harbors, Minnesota. I'll never forget how stunned I was at the sheer length of the machine!

In the upper peninsula of Michigan two short lines were on our route. The first was Escanaba & Lake Superior, but the line was already dieselized, and I settled for a photo of diesel switcher #101 pulling a train of wood pulp and paper cars out of a mill in Groos, Michigan. The Manistique and Lake Superior, later in the day, proved more to my liking. This short line was a subsidiary of the Ann Arbor Railroad at this time. At Manistique, proud little Consolidation #2380 was switching cars on weedy yard tracks.

MACKINAW CITY

We stopped for the night at Mackinaw City, Michigan. In 1951 both the New York Central and Pennsylvania maintained passenger train service into the city. On this night I found a Pennsy passenger train of nine cars laying over in the yards. At Elberta, Michigan, I added the Ann Arbor to my collection, getting a shot of 2-8-0 #2180 near the ferry landing.

As it turned out, this trip through the northlands was as interesting to me as any from a rail perspective.

Well groomed Mikado #401 of Green Bay & Western is spotted under the coal dock in Green Bay, Wisconsin. The road's 2-8-2s were the largest power on the roster and kept things moving on this east-west bridge route across the state.

173

RIGHT. Northern Pacific's famous streamliner, the *North Coast Limited,* begins to move out of St. Paul Union Station at 8:35 a.m. July 16, 1951. The husky EMD power has a 48-hour journey to Seattle ahead of it.

BELOW. On the morning of July 16, 1951, 4-8-4 #2675 rolls under Third Street in St. Paul with Northern Pacific's standard equipment *Alaskan.* Two years earlier I met #2675 at Billings, Montana with the westbound *Alaskan,* thus it was a pleasant surprise to see an old friend again.

BELOW. After bringing Northern Pacific's *Alaskan* into St. Paul Union Station, Northern #2675 scurried to Cayuga Street roundhouse where she was turned and is now being given a steam bath. The description "Northern" for a 4-8-4 locomotive came from Northern Pacific, as that road was the first to utilize this wheel arrangement during the 1920s.

Chicago & NorthWestern's *Mondamin* swings into St. Paul behind Pacific #503. Markings on the engine identify her as that of Chicago, St. Paul, Minneapolis & Omaha, the original official name for C&NW's line from St. Paul to Omaha. To C&NW folk, #503 is an "Omaha" engine.

ABOVE. When is the Burlington not the Burlington? When it's Rock Island's *Zephyr-Rocket* arriving at St. Paul in 1951! The joint Burlington-Rock Island streamliner used Burlington rails from St. Louis to Burlington, Iowa, then Rock Island trackage to St. Paul. The two roads also shared equipment and motive power on the *Zephyr-Rocket,* thus in this scene, despite a CB&Q diesel, the train is actually on Rock Island rails and is a Rock Island train!

BELOW. Unlike the previous page, there are no riddles here, for this is indeed the Burlington at St. Paul. Twin EMD units arrive with the long heavy *Blackhawk* from Chicago and rolling under Third Street Viaduct in 1951.

LEFT. Low-drivered Consolidation #2180 of Ann Arbor, owned by the Wabash, was found at Elberta, Michigan in July, 1951. Wabash buffs will recognize the parent's ancestry of #2180.

OPPOSITE PAGE, BELOW. On a summer day in 1951, 2-8-0 #2380 of Manistique & Lake Superior performs yard work at Manistique, Michigan. This short line in Michigan's Upper Peninsula was owned by the Ann Arbor.

BELOW. A Baldwin VO switcher of Escanaba & Lake Superior hauls a short consist of wood and paper products near Groos, Michigan in the twilight years of the Upper Peninsula's short lines.

Chapter Fifteen

Iowa Days

In the summer of 1948, after returning from the Great Graduation Trip mentioned in Chapters 9 and 10, I took a summer job as a clerk in a millwork factory near the Rock Island tracks in Peru, Illinois. A storeroom with an open door near the tracks was next to my room, and the whistle of an approaching Rock Island train would induce me to take a moment's break at the trackside door. The newest, and last, of Rock Island's steam power, ten R-67 Northerns built in 1946 and numbered 5110-5119, were used exclusively on the east end of the system.

These coal burning 4-8-4s ran mainly between Kansas City/Omaha and Chicago, while 10 oil burning Northerns numbered 5100-5109 built in 1944 were used west of Armourdale (Kansas City). Despite my admitted partiality to the Rock Island, I believe that the 5100 series Northerns were the most beautiful 4-8-4s in America. Their lines were clean and compact. They were fast, brawny engines with 74-inch drivers and 67,090 pounds of tractive effort.

OCCASIONAL DIESELS

In the summer of 1948 the Northerns were handling most of the heavy freight between Silvis and Burr Oak Yard in Blue Island, Illinois with only an occasional EMD F unit diesel making the run. I began at my factory to see if I could spot all 10 Northerns during the few weeks of my employment. I recorded their numbers on a pad as they passed each day, and finally I had all numbers listed except #5117, which never seemed to appear. I wondered if it was in the shop or used on night runs. On my last day at work, I was thrilled to see #5117 roar past on an eastbound fruit block.

My parents saw to it that I received a college education, and in September, 1948 I began my higher education at Cornell College in Mt. Vernon, Iowa. I soon found out that Iowa was surprisingly rich in rail activity and interest. Mt. Vernon, a small town some 15 miles east of Cedar Rapids, was on the main line of the Chicago & NorthWestern. Each day brought a constant parade of freight and passenger trains only two blocks from my college residence hall. By 1948 C&NW was dieselizing in earnest, yet steam still accounted for about 40% of all movements. Big 4-8-4s still hauled some of the freight, and cowled E-4 Hudsons pulled many of the secondary passenger trains. There was a long grade coming up into Mt. Vernon from the west, and many evenings I stood over the tracks on an old wooden country road bridge and watched a 4-8-4 with a long freight

With an extra west for Council Bluffs, a Rock Island R-67 class Northern awaits a green block at Iowa City in May, 1949. Many felt that the Rock's 5100 series Northerns were the most beautiful in the nation. Rock Island's debatable rush to dieselization in the early 1950's meant retiring and scrapping these great 4-8-4s far too early and quickly. I will add a sad postscript here; #5115, born April, 1946, died May, 1955. R.I.P.

CEDAR RAPIDS

On Saturdays, I often hitchhiked into Cedar Rapids with my camera in tow. This city was a great railroad town. The C&NW main line ran through Cedar Rapids, and all passenger trains, including the West Coast streamliners, stopped there. Additionally, Rock Island's busy line from West Liberty to St. Paul came through town, and a large yard and engine terminal were located on the north side of town. A visit to this yard in 1948 usually produced some new F-type diesel freight locomotives and, on the steam side, some 3000-series 2-10-2s and 5000-series Northern.

Branch lines of Illinois Central and Milwaukee also entered Cedar Rapids. For juice fans, the Cedar Rapids and Iowa City (CRANDIC), and the Waterloo, Cedar Falls and Northern were situated in Cedar Rapids as well.

My favorite routine in Cedar Rapids was to begin at the big passenger station which was shared by C&NW and Rock Island. I would then walk northward along the joint trackage used by these two lines plus the IC and Milwaukee. In a few blocks the C&NW tracks curved sharply away to the west and crossed the Cedar River. Near this location, C&NW maintained a small roundhouse which housed no main line power but only branch, yard and light duty engines.

Continuing on my walk I came next to an old Milwaukee engine shed and still further along, a small IC roundhouse. Both of these facilities were for branch line power only, so these walks usually revealed some interesting and unique species of old- and light-locomotives.

Proceeding further north I came to the big Rock Island facilities: Cedar Rapids was the hub of the road's Cedar Rapids division between St. Paul and Burlington, Iowa. In fact, many years earlier, Cedar Rapids was home to major Rock Island shops and a 49-stall roundhouse. In 1948 the house was down to 24 stalls, but Cedar Rapids was still a mighty busy spot on the Rock Island. The Rock was dieselizing a lot of its freight runs in 1948 but happily many were still coming into Cedar Rapids behind steam power, including the older 5000-series Northerns (Class R67-B) and 3000-series N-83 2-10-2s. The latter were favorite photo subjects of mine because Rock Island's Santa Fe's never were used east of Silvis across Illinois.

On the diesel side, three-unit EMD FTs and rare F2s made appearances at Cedar Rapids. In red and black paint schemes, RI's diesels were strikingly attractive.

ACTIVE JUNCTION

West Liberty lay a few miles southeast of Mt. Vernon, and for a Rock Island fan, this active junction point was a delight. Here at West Liberty, the Cedar Rapids division crossed the main line at the passenger station. Although this line was used by the *Zephyr-Rocket* between St. Louis and St. Paul, the primary purpose of this location was as a connection between the main line

Rock Island 2-10-2 #3029 brings a St. Paul-Chicago freight down the Cedar Rapids Division at West Liberty, Iowa on April 30, 1949. At West Liberty she will curve onto the main line towards Silvis yards. The N-83 class Santa Fes packed 77,700 pounds of tractive force, the largest on the Rock Island!

Here's 4500 hp of RI F-2 units at Cedar Rapids, Iowa in May, 1949 in an A-B-A configuration. Smoke in the background is not from a faulty unit on #47, but from a 4-8-4 on an adjacent track.

and the Cedar Rapids division. Freights from Chicago and Silvis swung off the main line on their way to Iowa Falls and St. Paul.

In 1948, Rock Island ran daily Chicago-St. Paul freights using West Liberty Junction. A day at this location produced a variety of steam and diesel motive power on both the main line and Cedar Rapids Division. In addition, a coaling dock was located at West Liberty, and nearly all freight locomotives stopped for coal and water.

One of my rare finds on the Cedar Rapids Division was T-31 4-6-0 #1581 at Cedar Rapids, one of only 10 4-6-0s left on the entire Rock Island by 1948! This locomotive was used on the light Decorah, Iowa branch.

On occasions when I returned home to La Salle, Illinois from college it was necessary to catch a Rock Island train at Iowa City, 20 miles south of Mt. Vernon. Since the road between Mt. Vernon and Iowa City was lightly used, it was less than an attractive hitchhiking venture, and I would often elect to hitchhike into Cedar Rapids on a much busier highway and take the Cedar Rapids and Iowa City interurban to Iowa City.

These pastoral occasions on the CRANDIC were typical of Midwestern interurban operations with street running, farm lane stops and roller coaster travel through woods and valleys.

In the spring of 1949 I took a C&NW train from Mt. Vernon to Marshalltown some 80 miles west, to photograph the Chicago Great Western and the Minneapolis & St. Louis. I had never seen the latter road and luckily there was a lot of M&StL action in town on that day. The railroad was close to full dieselization by then, and the line's two hotshot freights chanced to meet in Marshalltown that morning behind brand new F-7 units.

Happily, a secondary freight arrived behind one of M&StL's white-trimmed Mikados. CGW was quiet in Marshalltown on that morning except for the resident 0-6-0 switcher. My hope of catching one of CGW's big 2-10-4 types was not fulfilled but, all in all, Marshalltown provided a good series of photos.

In retrospect, Iowa produced an excellent portfolio of rail photos, and for a dedicated Rock Island fan like myself, it was a cornucopia of that railroad's motive power in the last days of steam and first days of the diesel.

An unusual Rock Island doubleheader is pictured at Cedar Rapids in May, 1949. The road engine is 2-10-2 #3014 and the helper is 4-6-2 #898. Both pull ahead for water after cutting off their train (in background). While rare for a Pacific to be used in freight service (and teamed with a Santa Fe), #898 is working her way to Chicago to spend the remaining four years in suburban service. A closer look at 2-10-2 #3014 is found in Chapter One, at Silvis, exactly one year to the month earlier.

ABOVE. Rock Island R-67B class Northern #5007, flying white "extra" flags, blows her steam cocks at Cedar Rapids in May, 1949. She's just gotten the green eye from the block signal and is beginning to roll with 76 cars of Silvis-bound freight.

OPPOSITE PAGE, TOP. C&NW 4-6-0 #1103 performs switching chores at the road's east yard in Cedar Rapids, May, 1949. As railroads began to dieselize branch lines with Geep units in the late 1940s, light steamers were transferred to various other duties, many to yard and terminal work such as shown here.

OPPOSITE PAGE, BOTTOM. One of only five Rock Island BL-2s, #427 takes a ride on the table at Cedar Rapids round-house in May, 1949. She's only four months old here and is assigned to the Cedar Rapids Division for local and light freight duties.

LEFT. Another lucky moment as two C&NW Mikados, with respective freights for Clinton and Omaha, pass on the east side of Marshalltown, Iowa in May, 1949, and both are moving!

LEFT. With a staccato barking of exhaust, C&NW E-4 Hudson #4002 storms out of the Marshalltown, Iowa station in 1949 with the eastbound *Los Angeles Limited.* The cowled, olive-green 4-6-4 has plenty of muscle to wheel the long, heavy train across the Midwest to Chicago. Oh, if one could but return to 1949, if just for a day!

Only a few days after the E-4 scene in Marshalltown, the westbound *Los Angeles Limited* scurries through Mt. Vernon, Iowa, this time however behind EMD units. By 1949, C&NW movements, both freight and passenger, were about evenly divided between steam and diesel. This evening portrait reveals the historic lefthand running of this railroad.

A Chicago Great Western brakeman rides the footboards of that road's Marshalltown, Iowa resident switcher. This study clearly shows the traditional emblem of "The Corn Belt Route" on the tender of the 0-6-0.

Neat 2-8-2 #609 of Minneapolis & St. Louis pauses at the yard office in Marshalltown, Iowa in May, 1949. Few other railroads, if any, applied white striping to everyday workhorse Mikados. I saw my first M&STL Mikado in Peoria in 1945 and was surprised at the semi-streamlined appearance of the line's freight locomotives.

Minneapolis & St. Louis F3 #147 takes a siding in Marshalltown, Iowa on October 7, 1948, with hotshot freight #20. This time-freight schedule had priority rights over all other trains (including passenger) except for its counterpart #19, which had rights over #20 because of direction. In this scene, #20 has indeed taken the siding to await a meet with #19.

My memories are filled with IC coal trains working through La Salle, Illinois. This photo, taken in 1944, shows Mikado #2119 southbound with a load of empty coal hoppers headed for southern Illinois. The lift bridge in the background (towers visible) was Burlington's Zearing-Streator branch over the Illinois River. Even though IC abandoned this line, the fill and track (now operated by a private industry) can still be seen today, but the Burlington bridge is gone.

Chapter Sixteen

Memories

As I conclude this book, it has been roughly 40 years since the events described herein took place. All that is left now are memories. There are no more whistles in the night, at least the kind I knew and loved so well. It was a fabulous era for a railfan, and often I wish for a time machine to take me back, if just for one day.

Here in Illinois most of the main lines still exist, but hundreds of miles of branch lines are gone forever. During the 40's, these branch and secondary lines were all active with daily freight trains and some passenger service. Now only weedy rights-of-way mark the places where tracks once ran. In many places nature has hidden all evidence of them.

Even today though, I still get a thrill from finding the evidence along highways and rivers. In many places crossings over abandonded roadbeds can still be found. In other places, old locomotive barns and tree-filled turntable pits can still be seen. Along back roads some railroad crossing signs still stand, rotting and ghostly, guarding nothing now but a patch in the blacktop where rails once existed. In other places, semaphore signals still stand along abandoned rights-of-way, somehow not removed when the rails were taken up. Some of them are rusted in the slow or clear position, commanding trains which will never come again except for those spectral engines which forever will work through the Illinois nights with beckoning whistles. Yes, it may all

RIGHT. At LaSalle, Illinois, limestone bridge piers of Burlington's abandoned Zearing-Streator line over the Illinois-Michigan canal still exist. Even through the 1940s this bridge saw several trains each day, including a passenger schedule of Pacific and coach, or gas-electric motor car.

LEFT. Between La Salle, Illinois and Utica lies Split Rock on the former RI main line. Before 1940, RI did not have enough space between the giant north rock and the I-M canal for both tracks of its main and thus bore a tunnel through the rock for its westbound track. In 1940, by filling in part of the long-abandoned canal, both tracks ran together to the south of the rock (left, in this photo) and the tunnel was abandoned. This 1989 photo shows the former RI (now CSX) track and the overgrown tunnel whose ceiling is today still stained with smoke of RI steam power.

RIGHT. RI's old freighthouse still stands in La Salle, Illinois. In the foreground is former RI main line now CSX. The Rock Island logo on the building, faded and weather worn, is still visible in this 1989 scene.

ABOVE. In June, 1989, this lonely semaphore still stood aside a long-abandoned IC right-of-way on the Champaign-Clinton branch. It protected a crossing of the Wabash at Lodge, Illinois (in background).

BELOW. There are still some sections of rail existing on the abandoned La Salle & Bureau County Railroad. This scene is north of Peru, Illinois, and as a youth I can recall LS&BC switching grain hoppers into the elevator in the distance.

be gone, but they cannot take the memories from me.

PUMPKINS AND TRAINS

My father, a University of Illinois alum, never missed the annual homecoming football game when I was young. This always meant an automobile trip from La Salle to Champaign in October with its gold and red plumage of maple and oak. It meant the unique aroma of burning leaves in small towns along the way. It meant red barns and corn shocks and farm stands which sold cider, pumpkins and gourds, and Indian corn. There is no place on earth like Illinois in October.

In addition, for me, it meant following the Illinois Central freight line down Route 51 from La Salle to Bloomington, where at least two or three coal trains behind 2-8-2s could be counted on along the way. In LaSalle, Minonk and Bloomington, limestone block engine barns were still in daily use. From Bloomington to Champaign the highway followed the Peoria and Eastern (New York Central) where I could always expect a freight behind a 4-8-2, as well as being passed by P&E's morning eastbound passenger train somewhere near LeRoy or Farmer City.

In Champaign I could count on seeing one of Illinois Terminal's orange electric interurban cars, and near the stadium itself, Illinois Central parked several football specials that traveled down from Chicago. Returning home in the darkness of an autumn evening, the whole process was repeated, with the delightful addition of the glow from a locomotive's firebox. The IC freight line is gone now, the rails removed several years ago, and the P&E (now Conrail) sees only rare traffic. Illinois Terminal is only a memory, and there are no more football specials on the IC.

Yet today, in my travels about Central Illinois, the evidence of better railroad days still can be found. The Illinois Terminal right-of-way and bridge piers are very obvious between Urbana and Danville and between Champaign and Decatur. In some stretches, the iron bolts which supported catenary are still imbedded in power poles, and many of Mr. McKinley's tile-roofed stations still stand in small towns. There are two spots in Champaign and one in Bloomington where IT's original rails still exist for a few feet, and the old Illinois Traction station still hands in its glory on University Avenue in Champaign, albeit long converted to businesses and offices. North of town, the turntable and a small section of the old IC roundhouse still exists.

In Villa Grove, the large Chicago & Eastern Illinois roundhouse stands in its entirety, and in Bloomington, Chicago & Alton's huge shop complex still exists in forlorn condition. The big Alton roundhouse is gone, but the circular concrete flooring is still there with rails showing in some spots.

As I drive through Central Illinois, I look for the evidence of how it once was and thrill to the memory of it all. In the summer of 1989, I went back to many of the old familiar places and photographed the evidence and memories which disappear more and more now with each passing year.

LEFT. The old Milwaukee depot still stands in Ladd, Illinois although all tracks are gone and the depot now houses another business. During the 1920s and '30s four passenger trains called here each day.

RIGHT. From this exact location atop the north portion of the Split Rock east of La Salle, Illinois the Illinois Valley Electric Railway bridged across to the man-made shelf on the south rock. The bridge carried interurbans across the Rock Island main line, the Illinois-Michigan Canal and towpath. The line was abandoned in the 1930s, track and bridge removed. Directly below was Rock Island's Split Rock Tunnel. Concrete abutments and iron bolts still exist on both rocks!

LEFT. What during the 1940s was a busy IC eight-track yard at LaSalle, Illinois was by 1989 only a weedy location. IC abandoned this freight line by 1975. Track in the foreground and hoppers in the distance belong to the Lone Star Corporation which brought three miles of the former IC line from their plant at Oglesby to a CSX connection at LaSalle. In the background, workers are dismantling the old IC enginehouse.

LEFT. A 4900 series 2-8-2 of the Burlington stands on permanent display on the far west side of Ottawa, Illinois. This particular Mikado served on the Aurora-Streater branch (through Ottawa), and thus it is fitting that it slumbers here.

RIGHT. A ghostly crossing sign still stands near White Heath, Illinois guarding nothing more now than patches across a country road where rails of both Illinois Central and Illinois Terminal once ran.

LEFT. Now completely filled with trees, an old Wabash turntable can be found in Forrest, Illinois. The operator's shanty still contains some rusted controls and wiring. Unused for 40 years, the table once turned engines used on the Streater branch as well as local division freight engines.

RIGHT. This Illinois Terminal bridge deck is still in excellent shape today although the IT has been gone for 35 years. Its location is just west of Seymour, Illinois.

LEFT. Several classic tile roof stations of the Illinois Terminal still stand in Central Illinois. Some of them, like this one in Bondville, were also power substations. At this location the IT track ran between the station and the building to the left.

RIGHT. This nostalgic photo shows the rear of an old Milwaukee enginehouse in Ladd, Illinois, still standing in 1989 (and probably today). Ladd was near the end of a meandering Milwaukee branch from Beloit. During the 1930s and '40s a light 2-8-2 was housed in this brick engine barn to work the Oglesby branch and the Cherry spur.

Epilogue

It is more than just how trains and railroads were a half century ago, for it coincided with a much more innocent and pure America. Those of us who grew up in small towns remember the ice cream socials on warm summer evenings with real honest-to-goodness homemade ice cream and lemonade. You sat on a bench near the band shell in the park with your girl and listened to the mournful song of the locusts in the mighty elms which was suddenly erased by the sound of the way freight blowing for Main Street crossing. Fathers took their youngsters down to the station on Saturdays, and we all set our watches *exactly* by the *Limited* roaring through town.

Some readers may never have seen a steam engine except in a movie or tourist museum, and may not conceive of how things were when railroads were in their glory days.

But you see, I knew, for I was there...and I am still there. Even today I can trace the old roadbed of the mysterious mining railroad called the Rutland, Toluca & Northern. I know a place deep in the green woods northwest of Toluca, Illinois where a person can still see the rotting ties and the limestone bridge piers of that rail line in a deep ravine. I can point out clear evidence in the older paved streets in Ottawa, Illinois where the rails of the Illinois Valley interurban once ran. And I know where a stone turntable pit of an old Chicago & NorthWestern branch still exists, deeply hidden in trees and bushes along Spring Creek at Spring Valley, Illinois.

When the diesels came something was lost forever, it seemed to me. Technology should replace convention and history it is claimed. But even that is suspect in my mind. I watch today as four Illinois Central diesel units groan and strain to get 80 empties out of Champaign, Illinois. I can remember when just *one* of IC's splendid 4-8-2s (always with that extra tender) would actually *accelerate* leaving town with 80 loaded coal hoppers. And I cannot forget a Nickel Plate Berkshire whipping through sleepy villages with a mile of freight at speeds greater than today's Amtrak passenger trains. I can remember that when a passenger train was behind schedule, the time was *made up* on the next division with no questions asked.

Why, I can recall my father giving up at 70 mph trying to pace a Peoria & Eastern passenger train between Farmer City and Mansfield, Illinois on single track behind a venerable 4-6-2.

You see, I can remember how it all was, and for me, those days of *real* trains are not gone at all. There is a truism that reads: *Everything that ever was, still is.* Yes, as long as there is memory and evidence, there is no doubt. That is what this book is all about.

Come visit me any summer night in Illinois. I'll take you to a spot where we can sit and smell the wet clover, and along about midnight we'll hear a lonely steam whistle. When we look across the glistening fields of corn, we'll see a ghostly headlight racing beneath the prairie moon.

Acknowledgements

Thanks to Donald J. Heimburger, railfan extraordinary publisher, fellow Illinoisan and friend, who had the insight to publish this book, despite the fact that it was different from the norm.

Thanks also to my cousin, Donald S. Charlton, of the University of Illinois, who accompanied me in tracking down age-old evidence, and whose professional expertise in construction and engineering verified the evidence beyond any doubt.

Heartfelt gratitude to my father, C.D. Charlton, one of the world's great men, who made it all possible, but who passed onto the last roundhouse before this book was published.

INDEX

Erwin, Tennessee, 160, 163, 167
Escanaba & Lake Superior Railroad, 173

F

Fairmont, West Virginia, 118
Farmer City, Illinois, 196
Fast Mail, 171
Flagstaff, Arizona, 153
Flemingsburg Junction, Kentucky, 108
Flemingsburg & Northern, 96, 108
Florida East Coast Railway, 65
Fordyce, Arkansas, 162
Fordyce & Princeton, 159, 162
Forrest, Illinois, 198
Fort Creve Coeur p. 28
Fox Indians, 93
Fredericksburg, Virginia, 137, 149
Freeport, Illinois, 10
Frisco, 78, 83, 84, 85, 102
Ft. Wayne, Indiana, 72
Ft. Worth, Texas, 85
Fulton, Kentucky, 102, 158, 159

G

Gadsden, Alabama, 160
Galesburg & Great Eastern, 87, 88, 89
Galesburg, Illinois, 14, 15, 29, 32, 75, 87
Gary, Indiana, 58, 63, 72, 120
General, 58, 64, 72
Geneva, Illinois, 69
George Washington, 107
Gilman, Illinois, 94
Golden State Limited, 8, 58, 62
Grand Canyon, 153, 154
Grand Canyon Limited, 22, 75, 103
Grand Central Station, 38, 40, 49, 54, 55
Grand Rapids, Michigan, 54
Grand Trunk Railroad, 37
Grand Trunk Western, 45, 46, 69, 101
Great Falls, Montana, 155
Great Northern Railway, 155, 171, 162
Great Western Railway, 152
Green Bay & Western Railroad, 170, 173
Green Bay, Wisconsin, 170, 173
Green Diamond, 20
Greenbrier, West Virginia, 163
Greenwood, Kentucky, 117
Groos, Michigan, 173, 181
Gulf, Mobile & Ohio Railroad, 18, 19, 21, 23, 24, 25, 26, 27, 76, 99

H

Hammond, Indiana, 39, 42, 53
Havana, Illinois, 87
Hessville, Indiana, 102
Hiawatha, 69, 171
Hiawatha-North Wood Section, 171
Hodge, Louisiana, 161
Holbrook, Arizona, 143
Hooppole, Illinois, 90, 91, 93
Hooppole, Yorktown & Tampico Railroad, 90, 91, 92, 93
Houston, Texas, 82

I

Illinois Central electric, 37
Illinois Central Iowa Division, 40
Illinois Central Railroad, 10, 17, 19, 20, 21, 22, 24, 25, 38, 40, 49, 69, 73, 75, 87, 89, 99, 158, 159, 160, 184, 194, 196, 197, 198
Illlinois Division, 16
Illinois-Michigan Canal, 6, 195, 197
Illinois Midland, 87

Illinois Northern Railway, 38
Illinois River, 8, 10, 17, 20, 87, 194
Illinois Terminal Railroad, 18, 19, 20, 21, 28, 196, 198, 199
Illinois Traction System, 6, 196
Illinois Valley Division, 6, 10
Illinois Valley Electric Railway, 197
Imperial, 67
Indiana Harbor Belt Railroad, 20, 37
Indianapolis, Indiana, 19, 21
Inter City Limited, 134
Interstate Express, 63
Iowa City, Iowa, 7, 183, 184, 185
Iowa Falls, Iowa, 156, 185
Ivy City Terminal, 136, 144, 145, 149

J

Jersey City, New Jersey, 135, 136, 141, 142, 145
Jersey City Terminal, 136, 145
Jim Crow, 163
Joliet, Illinois, 22, 27, 65, 66, 75
Joliet Union Station, 19, 22, 27

K

Kankakee, Illinois, 19, 20, 22, 23, 26, 69, 75
Kansas City, Kansas, 20, 29, 182
Kansas City Southern Railway, 159, 165
Katy Flyer, 78, 79
Kearney, Nebraska, 152
Kensett, Arkansas, 161
Kensington, Illinois, 73
Kentucky & Indiana Terminal Railroad, 113
Kentucky & Tennessee Railway, 114, 115
Kewaunee, Green Bay & Western Railroad, 170
Knickerbocker, 79
Knoxville, Tennessee, 95

L

La Grange works, 44
La Salle & Bureau County Railroad, 10, 26, 87, 89, 196
La Salle, Illinois, 6, 7, 10, 11, 16, 17, 21, 26, 76, 87, 89, 94, 185, 194, 195, 197
La Salle Street Station, 38, 39, 56, 71
Lackawanna River, 137
Lackawanna & Wyoming Valley interurban, 136, 140
Ladd, Illinois, 10, 21, 26, 87, 89, 197, 199
Lake Cities, 50
Lake Forest, Illinois, 172
Latrobe, Pennsylvania, 118, 129
Laurel Line, 136, 140
Le Roy, Illinois, 196
Lebanon, Indiana, 94, 96, 97
Lederer Iron & Steel Co., 104
Lehigh Valley Railroad, 134, 135, 136, 138
Lexington, Kentucky, 96, 104
Liberty Limited, 60, 62
Ligonier Valley Railroad, 118, 129
Lima, Ohio, 21, 27
Lima-Peoria branch, 30
Little Englewood Station, 38, 49, 74
Lodge, Illinois, 196
Logansport, Indiana, 92, 94, 96
Lone Star Corporation, 197
Los Angeles, California, 67, 154
Los Angeles Limited, 191
Los Angeles Union Passenger Terminal, 156
Los Angeles Union Station, 154
Louisiane, 49, 75
Louisville, Kentucky, 52, 65, 113
Louisville & Nashville Railroad, 65, 95, 96, 97, 98, 108, 159, 160
Louisville, New Albany & Corydon Railroad, 164, 168

Loveland, Colorado, 152

M

Mackinaw City, Michigan, 163
Manhattan, New York, 136
Manistique & Lake Superior Railroad, 173, 181
Manistique, Michigan, 173, 181
Manufacturer's Junction, 38
Maple Leaf, 46, 69
Marshalltown, Iowa, 185, 191, 192, 193
McGuire-Cummings, 28
McKinley, William B., 196
Meadow River Lumber Railroad, 164
Meadowlark, 43, 48, 156
Memphian, 83
Memphis, Tennessee, 160
Mendota, Illinois, 10, 12, 14
Mercury, 73
Meteor, 78, 84
Miami, Florida, 65, 95
Michigan Central, 73, 132
Middletown & New Jersey Railway, 141
Middletown, New York, 141
Middletown & Unionville Railway, 141
Midland Terminal, 153
Midlander, 51
Midnight, 74
Miller Park, 30
Millington, Illinois, 87
Milwaukee Road, 19, 26, 37, 69, 70, 87, 105, 171, 172, 184, 197, 199
Milwaukee, Wisconsin, 69, 70, 172
Minneapolis & St. Louis, 185, 192, 193
Minot, North Dakota, 172
Mission Tower, 154
Mississippi Railway, 102
Missouri-Kansas-Texas Railroad, 78, 79, 83
Missouri Pacific Railroad, 44, 78, 80, 82, 101, 152, 156, 159, 161, 162
Missourian, 78
Mixed Train Daily, 86
Moberly Division, 35
Modesto, California, 155, 156
Moffat Tunnel, 155
Mondamin, 176
Monon, 37, 38, 39, 42, 48, 52, 53
Monongahela Railroad, 118
Morehead, Kentucky, 110
Morehead & North Fork Railroad, 96, 110
Morning Daylight, 156
Morning Hiawatha, 70
Morning Star, 78
Morning Zephyr, 70
Morris, Illinois, 8
Mt. Vernon, Iowa, 182, 184, 185, 191

N

Nashville, Chattanooga & St. Louis, 160
Nashville, Tennessee, 159, 164
Negley, Ohio, 120, 130
New England States, 62
New Lisbon, Wisconsin, 171
New Orleans, Louisiana, 49, 159, 160, 165
New River, Tennessee, 115, 117, 118
New York Central, 19, 26, 37, 38, 56, 57, 58, 59, 62, 63, 66, 69, 71, 73, 79, 87, 98, 109, 132, 173, 196
New York Central's Kankakee Belt Route, 26
New York City, New York, 56, 136, 142
Newark, Illinois, 87
Niagara, 58, 71
Niagara Falls, 132, 134
Nickel Plate, 19, 21, 27, 30, 37, 38, 56, 57, 58, 62, 64, 102, 104
Nickel Plate Limited, 62